DEDICATION

To all those who endured growing up in the care system, your stories matter, and your resilience is a testament to the human spirit. And to those tragically who did not survive, may this book honour your memory and shine a light on the injustices you suffered.

A TAYLOR

CONTENTS

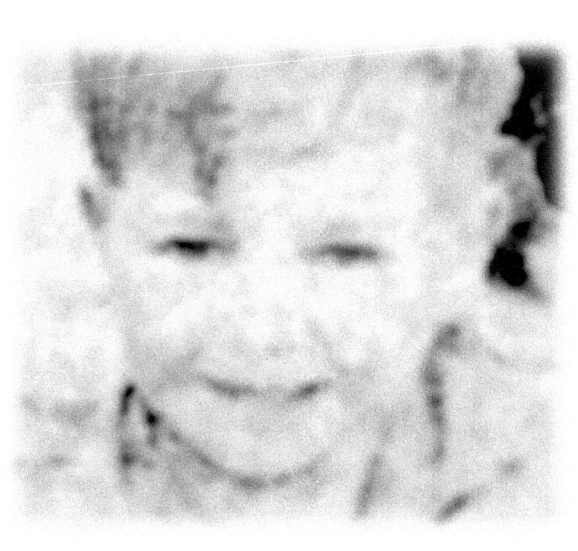

PROLOGUE:
INTO THE UNKNOWN

On a cool autumn night in 2005, I stood on a bridge and watched the calm light dance upon the river, a stark contrast to my tumultuous inner world. The serene glimmer of the water mirrored Belfast's city lights, a beautiful irony to the hurricane raging within my mind. A relentless internal dialogue churned, grappling with the immense pain and suffering that had become my constant companions.

"I can't bear this any longer," I confessed to the night, my voice barely a whisper. The weight of my internal struggle was becoming unbearable.

Guilt and shame, those relentless shadows of my past, mingled with the fresh remorse of the present. I had tasted success, but it had all come crashing down like a house of cards. My career and my marriage had suffered and surrendered to the ghostly chains of my past. In gambling, I had sought to fill a void, only to find deeper desolation. It seemed that the place that had stolen my childhood had come back to claim victory in the end.

For years, I had locked away my true self, concealed my story in the deepest recesses of my soul, and now, perched precariously on the bridge's edge, the floodgates of my emotions burst open.

The pain was insurmountable, and in that distorted moment, it whispered a seductive lie – ending it all was the only escape.

It seemed that my journey had reached its terminal. The agony I bore had triumphed. In the depths of despair, I reasoned – no more shame, no guilt, no further pain for my family. I thought they would find peace in my absence, for I believed I offered nothing but disappointment.

The onslaught of fear, anxiety, and memories pummelled my spirit relentlessly. My life's rollercoaster – the hyper-vigilance, the skirmishes with inner demons – had brought me to this point. The cascade of emotions, so intense and overpowering, overshadowed any logic or thought of the devastation I would leave behind. At that moment, I was engulfed by the storm within.

It was a battle of epic proportions, waged in the confines of my mind, a fight between the remnants of good in my life and the excruciating evil of pain. And in that hour, the anguish was so profound that it threatened to obliterate all traces of light.

The complexity of the mind is such that in its darkest moments, it amplifies pain until it becomes all-consuming. It was this overwhelming desire to end the pain that had brought me to the edge, to the brink of making an irreversible decision. The distortions laboured by alcohol and mental turmoil had forged chains too heavy to bear.

In those moments of contemplating the unthinkable, the pain was not just a whisper but a deafening roar, and on that day, it seemed to have claimed victory.

The stigma of mental ill-health, a heavy cloak I had worn for too long, kept my deepest thoughts and scars hidden in the shadows.

As I sat there, on the edge of the bridge, my phone rang incessantly. A friend desperately trying to reach me. Her words, filled with fear and concern, spoke of alternatives, of hope yet unseen. But I was paralysed, a prisoner of my own tumultuous emotions. At that harrowing crossroads, I was overwhelmed by an urge to end my life, to cease the relentless chains that bound me. Rational thought had abandoned me, leaving me adrift in a sea of fight-or-flight instinct.

Never did I consider the consequences of my potential leap, the gaping void I would leave in the lives of those I loved. All that consumed me was the need to extinguish the agony within. I felt like a failure, haunted by the spectres of a childhood marred by trauma. With its cold walls and colder hearts, Nazareth House had instilled a sense of worthlessness that now echoed loudly in my head. "I tried, I really did try," I thought, but to me, it had never been enough.

This was the depth of despair I had reached, the worst moment of a life tormented by past and present demons. And yet, it was not the end. From this abyss, I found a path – rugged and steep – leading me to places of healing and understanding. This is not just a story of despair; it is a chronicle of rising out of the depths of misery and constant struggle, a testimony to the resilience of the human spirit and the transformative power of healing.

My lifeline came not from within but from the outside – a voice that reached through the noise of my despair. The arrival of the police and the ensuing conversations with psychiatric nurses were all lifelines thrown into the turbulent waters of my psyche.

Yet, even in those moments of rescue, I held back the full truth, shrouded by the immense shame that clung to me like a second skin.

In the pages that follow, I invite you to journey with me to the brink of that bridge and then on to a place of recovery, understanding, hope, and acceptance of mental health struggles. It is a story of resilience and hope for anyone who has ever felt lost in the dark shadows of life, for it is in our darkest moments that we often discover the most enduring light.

CHAPTER 1:

IMPENDING GLOOM

In the northeast of Scotland lies the Silver City by the North Sea – Aberdeen - renowned for its silver granite buildings and oceanic climate with a busy seaport. Here stood Nazareth House, a colossal building in grey granite that bore the weight of a century on Claremont Street. It was an imposing structure, with intricate carvings on its facade and numerous sash windows, which had withstood the tests of time, harbouring tales of desolation behind its sombre walls.

The entrance to Nazareth House was through a gatehouse on the periphery of the building. At the centre of the pointed archway was the date '1871' engraved in stone.

Each return through that archway revived a lingering dread within me. I vividly remember the unwavering sense of foreboding as I passed beneath the engraved year of establishment. No matter the distance travelled, or the brief escapes, crossing that threshold always signified a return to an overshadowed existence.

The number was etched in my mind as the bus used to stop outside the gates, and we had to walk through the pointed archway to enter the house and walk up to the massive building. There was always a sense of dread or fear coming back through those gates – no matter where I had been. The date engraved on that archway was something I would glance up at – and was the last thing of the 'outside world' that my gaze would hold onto before facing the onslaught that was my life inside.

At the back of the building, there used to be a door and a corridor that led to the laundry rooms. I remember once being led along that corridor and out into the quadrangle and the nuns using my own shoe to beat me black and blue for wetting the bed again.

An expansive building, it was built in the late 19th century, and it appeared to have withstood the test of time. Its imposing exterior was covered with intricate stonework with many sliding sash windows. It furnished itself with an air of sombre overbearing ambience. The house's interior had a completely irregular pattern of what seemed miles of corridors, with many nooks and crannies that I'm sure held many secrets locked in its passageways for years, well before I arrived as a two-year-old boy in 1963.

In those early years, the corridors made no sense, and I felt lost. It was an overwhelming feeling. I was never taken by the hand and lead around, nor was I ever picked up. It seemed so dark, and scary – it was overwhelmingly huge.

The entrance to Nazareth House had a parlour on each side of the entrance, which led to a small corridor into the main reception area and chapel, which had two sets of staircases on either side. They were not grand staircases, which you might have expected, but more functional than anything else. To the left of the main reception area was a door that led you to a lift and the elderly accommodation. In Nazareth House at the time – there was a boy's side, a girl's side and elderly/infirm residents. The nun's accommodation was to the right of the main reception area. You were never allowed in there - it was a no-go area.

It most definitely gave a vibe of being haunted from an aesthetic point of view, both inside and out.

I remember once, around the age of 7, I received a birthday present from my mother. I also had a telephone call from her – the one and only time we spoke whilst there. As a result, I was allowed into the nun's accommodation to receive the call. I had to go down a passageway past their dining room, and into an informal office where I got to take the call. My mother wished me a happy birthday and that is all I can remember of the call.

I found out many years later that my mother had been unable to cope and had asked an aunt to look after me and my brother. My mother sadly never returned to collect us, and as a consequence, Social Services were contacted, and we were placed in short-term foster care, although I have no recollection of those early years. We were then admitted to Nazareth house when I was 2 years old.

I was informed many years later that my mother had a very cold persona and my father drank a lot and had been in and out of prison for petty crime. My mother apparently spent many years being pregnant and had a tough life, and I have no doubt, having had a large family, she probably suffered from mental health issues.

The building whispered tales of forgotten innocence with its darkly lit corridors, constantly feeling very cold and eerie when you walked along them, a very daunting experience for any child.

In the winter, in particular, you could visualise your breath as you expelled it into the air no matter what time of day it was that cold. The silence was unnerving, with weird shadows on the walls casting non-descriptive shapes that appeared to dance, always having the ability to take your breath away whenever you noticed them.

As a child it was a frightening experience and felt as if a scary monster or ghost could jump out at you anytime. I would walk very slowly along those corridors, my heart pounding and with trepidation, as I always felt so frightened, not knowing what might be ahead. It would be terrifying for any adult, let alone a child. Fear most definitely became the norm for me as a two-year-old infant and growing into an older child. It never left me. Little did I know this was to be my home for the next twelve years of my life.

.oOo.

My most vivid childhood memory is riding a small, shiny, red tricycle around a concrete playground devoid of any grass at the rear of a towering building. I must have felt bewildered, plucked from a home I no longer recall and placed into this cold, concrete environment. The building behind me loomed ominously, but I relished the freedom of riding my tricycle outside, doing what I wanted on my own.

In the middle of the playground stood a tall metal maypole, surrounded by two sets of rusty old play equipment, each set with three swings, and an old merry-go-round. This bleak playground was enveloped by the massive grey structure known as Nazareth House. Despite the stark surroundings, I probably felt a sense of freedom, riding around the playground for hours, unaware of the future impact of being there.

Even at that young age, I had the ability to compartmentalise my thoughts and feelings, hiding them in metaphorical boxes deep in my mind, hoping they would remain closed forever.

Nazareth House Aberdeen was run by the Poor Sisters of Nazareth, a Catholic order founded in 1851 with the Vatican's approval. They built homes for the homeless, destitute children, and the elderly.

Upon entering Nazareth House, you were directed to one of two parlours located on either side of the entrance. I vividly remember my first meeting in the front parlour of Nazareth House in Aberdeen. These parlours, filled with the finest furniture and treasures, exuded a sense of opulence. The room was adorned with lush velvet-coloured chairs and an exquisite shiny mahogany table at its centre, complemented by a matching mahogany sideboard. Velvet curtains dressed the large sash windows, adding warmth and brightness to the room and creating a vibrant and happy atmosphere.

It didn't matter what religion you were - protestant or catholic - you were indoctrinated and bible bashed into the beliefs of the catholic church. To this day, I still hold a loathing and distaste for the catholic church and the way they protected so many abusers. They were in complete denial regarding their punitive practices against innocent children worldwide. Hate is a strong word but in this case there is no other word to describe the Vatican and its practice of cover ups.

As a child, I had no idea where I was or what was happening. I recall a stern-looking nun instructing me not to touch anything. She stood there in her black and white habit, with chains around her waist and a large crucifix hanging from a long chain, exuding an air of authority and power. This was my first face-to-face encounter with a nun, and it was far from pleasant. The experience was intimidating and frightening as I looked up at her emotionless face.

Throughout those years, I thought they all looked like penguins, though they were certainly neither cute nor cuddly.

Little did I know this was the start of my journey which would be filled with unhinged emotion in this thing we called life.

CHAPTER 2:

COMFORTING FRESH LINEN

Although my life had taken an unexpected turn, I hope to convey the resilience within me to inspire others that you can overcome trauma, find contentment, and achieve success, as I did with a career in the Army followed by a career in Social Work.

Throughout this memoir, I have not specified my age during certain incidents, as it's impossible to be precise. The detailed memory of the front parlour, for example, is vivid because over the twelve years I was at Nazareth House, I was frequently summoned there. Visitors were entertained in that room, where the best of everything was displayed, from fine china to historically rich furniture.

I had many solemn encounters with the stern nun who chastised me verbally on my first visit to the parlour. These interactions, like many others, left a lasting impression.

The stark contrast between the opulent parlour and the day-to-day life at Nazareth House was striking. One example that comes to mind is the bedding we were given: a lumpy pillow, two starched white sheets, a plain white pillowcase, and a scratchy grey blanket that felt awful against the skin.

However, the bedding we used daily was replaced with luxurious bedspreads whenever visitors came. This deception created an illusion of a bright, happy environment, hiding the harsh reality we lived in. Once the visitors left, the bedding was immediately changed back – in order to be fresh for the next time it might be needed.

The laundry, however, was a haven of warmth and comfort. Rows of metal contraptions dried the laundry, and the smell of freshly washed linen always gave me a sense of calm.

The laundry was a separate building backing onto the playground. I would sneak in there on cold days to warm up and find comfort. It was like a holiday retreat, with the fresh linen and warmth making me feel at ease. I would hide under a small table, often left unsupervised in the yard.

Nothing bad ever happened in the laundry. I never got caught because there was a side door the nuns didn't use. I could see them coming and would crawl out on my hands and knees. The churning cylinders and noise gave me an overwhelming sense of relaxation. It was my favourite place, especially in autumn and winter, a sanctuary from the silence and cold outside.

Unbeknownst to me at the time, the playground backed onto a mortuary where dead nuns were embalmed before being laid to rest in the Chapel. This discovery added to my daily anxiety. Growing up under these conditions was far from typical.

Despite the trauma, I still love fresh linen on my bed, as it reminds me of the comfort I found in the laundry. I made sure no one else knew about my safe space and was careful not to spend too long there in case I was noticed missing. Once, someone tried to follow me, but I turned back to protect my secret haven.

Friendships were scarce as everyone dealt with their own inner turmoil. I was quite withdrawn, though social work reports claimed I always had a smile on my face. This was a coping mechanism to hide my inner turmoil and anxiety that I felt daily. Underneath it all, I was very scared. Bullying was prevalent, but it was nothing compared to the nuns' punitive regime and aggression.

I don't recall anyone my age, I must have been one of the youngest and myself and my brother were kept together with my sister. There were two sides male and female but because we were so young we were kept with my sister. She was always kind and protective even though she had her own struggles. I can't remember my relationship with her as such, and I didn't really grasp she was my sister until a long time later, as my level of understanding came to the fore. When she left at sixteen I was moved to the male side of the house. Although she promised to visit she struggled on the outside with minimal support back then.

In the male side of the house life was different. The older boys were all on survival mode, and the day–to–day life was difficult, with bullying being the norm.

School was also very challenging as we were perceived as outsiders no one really liked us.

Each day, on return from school, my job was to polish everyone's shoes for the next day, followed by homework, playtime, supper and bedtime. It was a very strict regime and punishments were harsh. If, for example, someone broke a window, we all were made to kneel on the floor, with our hands on the back of our heads, until someone confessed. If someone did admit to it the guilty party was punished and isolated.

Some of the nuns were particularly harsh with physical discipline.

Things improved significantly in or around 1973 when the nun who had been looking after us was replaced by someone new. From then on, the quality of life started to improve, and there was a shift in the regime throughout. Many of the old practices seemed to disappear slowly over a period of time.

CHAPTER 3:

NIGHTTIME TRAUMA

As a child, my very existence revolved around constant fear and anxiety. I remember standing in a metal cot, crying for what felt like hours because there was no one else in the room when I woke up.

I likely rocked myself to sleep many times, overwhelmed by the prolonged periods of isolation. On the second floor, without sleeping monitors, I felt utterly isolated, scared, and withdrawn. Over the years, I developed the ability to emotionally shut down, although as a child, I wasn't conscious of doing so.

Growing up there, I quickly learned that affection was non-existent. There were no hugs, no nurturing— such gestures simply weren't part of their nature. I recall trying to tug at a nun's habit to gain attention at a very young age, only to be rejected. I soon realised that seeking affection was futile. This rejection was hard to bear as a child, but it became the norm for me over time.

Rejection in any form has a profoundly negative impact, especially on a child institutionalised in such a brutal environment. It became a part of who I was, almost as if it were engraved on my soul. I never knew any different. It wasn't that I accepted it—I just had no choice. It was something you got used to, leaving you with an intense feeling of never being good enough, a pervasive sense of inadequacy that affected many children in the care system.

The evening routine was consistent and rigid. Someone would shout "suppertime," and we would come running from all directions. Suppertime was chaotic and always carried a sense of urgency, with the constant threat of consequences if you were late. I dreaded it because we were given a plastic mug of steaming hot cocoa, which had to be drunk quickly. In my haste, I often burned my lips or throat, fearing punishment for being too slow.

After supper, we were escorted to the bathroom to brush our teeth. There was no consideration for age or understanding; we were all treated the same. Once in bed, we had to adopt a position with our arms crossed over our upper bodies. We weren't allowed to move, but years later, I realised it was to prevent us from touching ourselves.

Once settled, the nun in charge would come around and recite a nighttime prayer repeatedly: "Now I lay myself down to sleep, I pray the Lord my soul to keep, but if I die before I wake, I pray the Lord my soul to take." This prayer, ingrained in my memory, was meant to instil fear, reminding us that we would burn in hell as punishment for our behaviours. This fear was very real to me as a child.

As children, we were naive and innocent, clueless about the religion imposed on us. My anxiety and fear were constant, manifesting in nightly bedwetting for years. This only heightened my anxiety and caused me to become very withdrawn.

It's difficult to describe the constant anxiety that weighed on me every second of every day. As a child, it felt like a heavy weight pressing down on my chest, sometimes taking my breath away. This anxiety was ever-present, though I didn't understand its cause. I likely experienced many anxiety attacks during my formative years.

To my credit, I later discovered a deep-rooted resilience within me. This resilience allowed me to function despite the trauma I had endured, a testament to the strength I found within myself.

CHAPTER 4:

EVIL PERSONIFIED

On most nights my sleep was interrupted by nuns waking me to go to the toilet at least once in the early hours. Later I would end up waking myself with that dreaded wet feeling, as I realised I had wet the bed again. On most occasions, the orange rubber sheet just wasn't enough. This of course interrupted my sleep so I had very little proper rest - so insomnia was part of growing up. I always had that dreaded feeling in the morning when daylight broke, as I knew what was coming.

Staring out the sash white windows as dawn was breaking I contemplated what lay ahead. On most mornings, and I remember them vividly, once it was time to get up I did so and I knew the routine very well. I had to remove my wet sheets and place them above my head, it was degrading and humiliating. I remember a feeling of confusion, apprehension and fear.

I then had to join the other bedwetters; the feeling of absolute dread would almost put me in a trance-like state as I prepared myself mentally, telling myself yet again it would all be over soon. The total humiliation that I felt when doing this was beyond whatever you could imagine.

The nuns would actively encourage other children to call you names to humiliate you further and with that became the overwhelming feeling of guilt and shame.

I constantly would question whether it was my fault and whether I could have prevented it. In fact maybe I deserved the beatings!

In anyone's childhood you always question why? For me I know I most definitely shut down and emotionally detached myself from what was happening. I couldn't describe to you as a child what I was doing but as an adult that's exactly what was happening. It was a coping mechanism, to deal with the confusion at the violence being inflicted on me. Believing in some way I had caused it, it was my fault yet again - my total naivety as a child.

As usual, I was grabbed by the ear and dragged up the corridor, accompanied by a torrent of abuse from the nun and the jeering catcalls of the other children. "How dare you wet the bed, you dirty little boy. Now everyone can see what you are, a dirty little boy that wets the bed." These words rang in my ears, repeated over and over, searing themselves into my memory and staying with me for years. The constant ridicule took its toll, affecting me more deeply than I could have ever imagined.

The verbal abuse was harrowing, but it came with an even greater sense of impending doom, knowing that punches would soon follow. This chaotic and abusive routine left me frozen, trying to cope with a million thoughts racing through my mind. Over time, I became numb to it all. The punches always targeted my torso or legs, never my face, though I was occasionally slapped. I would cry out as the punches continued with brutal force.

Then came the ultimate humiliation—being ordered to strip, stripping away my dignity along with my clothes, before being thrown into a cold bath. I didn't fight back or defend myself. Having grown up with this routine, I accepted it as an unchangeable part of my life.

Once in the bathroom, the pungent smell of Jeyes Fluid filled the air as the cold bath water mixed with the powerful disinfectant. One that is generally used for unblocking drains or disinfecting driveways. Then this irritant was poured over my body. The scrubbing that followed caused pain and a stinging sensation all over me, including my eyes. This practice still haunts me to this day. This was evil personified. How could anyone inflict such damage on any child?

As I grew older, I became increasingly numb to this process, not realising that this cruelty would have such a profound effect on my mental health in later years. Even as an adult, the deep sense of shame and guilt from this abuse never truly leaves you.

The verbal abuse, coupled with physical punishment, created an environment of constant terror. Each night, I lay awake, dreading the inevitable, my mind a whirlpool of fear and confusion. The routine became a grotesque form of normalcy, and I adapted by shutting down emotionally. This was my coping mechanism, my way of surviving the unbearable.

I remember vividly the nun's face, twisted with disdain, as she berated me. The words were like daggers, piercing my young, fragile heart. The other children's laughter added to my humiliation, making me feel isolated and alone. The communal scorn reinforced the message that I was worthless, reinforcing the belief that I deserved the pain and suffering inflicted upon me.

The physical pain was intense, but it was the emotional scars that cut the deepest. The icy bath, combined with the harsh scrubbing, felt like an assault on my very soul. The smell of Jeyes Fluid is forever etched in my memory, a symbol of the cruelty I endured. The ritual was a methodical stripping away of my humanity, designed to break my spirit. And it did.

Over time, I developed a resilience, a hard shell that allowed me to endure. But beneath that shell was a child, desperate for love and acceptance, struggling to understand why this was happening. The coping mechanisms I developed—emotional shutdown and detachment—were necessary for survival but came at a great cost.

CHAPTER 5:

SCHOOL

We were never educated within Nazareth House; instead, we were bussed out to school. One of the routines leading up to getting on the bus after breakfast was having our hair combed or brushed. For a few nuns, this was another opportunity to dish out more aggression. I remember standing there as a small boy, frozen to the spot as I queued for my turn. The slightest movement from me, and I'd feel a pair of knuckles rapped on the back of my head, a very painful experience. By this point in the morning routine, the nuns' frustration and anger had reached a boiling point.

Once your hair was plastered with Brylcreem and combed, you had to join another queue. This one was to receive your daily dose of malt or cod liver oil, both absolutely revolting in taste. On many occasions, like any child would, I gagged on them and often ended up being sick. You were forced to take whichever was available every morning.

I hated the morning routine. Even on a school day, my anxiety levels must have been sky-high. From being woken at 6am and enduring the wet bed routine, with the violence and trauma of constantly being in fear, it's no surprise that I have mental health issues today.

Once we boarded the double-decker bus, I don't remember much of the journey other than the street names - as I had learned them over many years. With my short legs dangling over the bus seat, I just used to stare out the windows, lost in a million thoughts of what would come from the day ahead, as a very young, confused boy full of anxiety.

It didn't take me long to realise that we were seen as different from the other kids at school. They called us the 'Nazees' because we were from Nazareth House, and everyone else we encountered called us 'outsiders.'

My school days weren't much better than other days. Like most children, there were many opportunities for bullies to take advantage, and they did. We were also seen as 'minks,' a term meaning individuals with poor hygiene or a smelly person. The irony of being called that, knowing I had been scrubbed with Jeyes Fluid earlier to clean me, angered me. If only they had known.

On top of the name-calling, like many others from the home, I received threats, punches, and kicks. One thing that probably identified us more than others was that we wore hand-me-downs, great ammunition for the outsiders.

The most humiliating experience I endured was when I was given a duffel coat one weekend by a particular nun as a winter coat. It had been donated along with other items by some family that weekend. I was delighted because winter had set in and it was very cold. That Monday was no different from any other. Once off the bus, I made my way to the playground and then to the cloakroom once the bell rang. I heard a group of boys laughing and relaying some story. One of the boys shouted to another, "Get his coat off!"

This resulted in a verbal exchange between us as he grabbed the coat off my back, belittling me in front of all his friends. To my horror, he pointed out his name stitched into the coat. He recognized it because his mother had handed it into Nazareth House. The chances of him recognising it were slim, but that's exactly what happened. This added fuel to the fire, and I was called names for months after. We ultimately ended up fighting and both ended up in the headmaster's office, where we were given three strikes by a Lochgelly Tawse, a strap with two or three tails at one end.

I often wondered why I deserved all the physical abuse whether at school or when I returned. It did give me a feeling of being unworthy with massive low self-esteem setting in very early in my younger years. Little did I know how my past would have a devastating impact on me later in life.

Once we returned from school, we had to immediately complete any homework. As a young boy,

I remember a particular nun sitting with me to do my reading on my return. The book was called 'Tip,' about the adventures of a small dog. This particular nun was very old, with a harsh and cold persona. She was intimidating and had a no-nonsense attitude. My dealings with her, like with most nuns, were filled with fear and trepidation. Doing my reading homework was no different.

Looking back, I probably stuttered through some sentences in fear of getting any words wrong, knowing that her way of dealing with mistakes was to hit you over the knuckles with a wooden ruler. This happened many times. It's unbelievable to think that their way of controlling us was through fear, not nurture, and with zero empathy or compassion.

This is something I have struggled with for many years. I often longed to ask them why they inflicted so much damage on children, both physically and mentally. Why did they choose fear over kindness, and control over care? The answers, I know, will never come, but the questions remain a part of my journey towards healing.

CHAPTER 6:

DEHUMANISED

Like most children, I looked forward to mealtimes as a break from the monotony of the day. If you were hungry, you ate whatever was put in front of you. We knew full well that a certain nun had a particular way of dealing with you if you didn't finish everything on your plate. The portions weren't large, but we knew no different, so we accepted what we were given or at least tried to.

Mealtimes were a strict regime filled with coercive control and manipulation. Some of us had to set the tables in advance, which involved laying out tablecloths and cutlery. The dining room was a fairly large space with a small kitchen annexed to it. A hatch connected the kitchen to the dining room, where food was served. I always remember how big the windows were, making the room bright, especially on sunny days when the sunlight would beam through and almost blind you.

The routine was always conducted in silence under the watchful eye of a sister. When everyone was called for dinner, we sat around the tables, and the sister would say grace, a prayer thanking God for the food. We were then allowed to queue up to receive our food. Speaking was strictly forbidden; any chatter would result in a slap or punishment later. Mealtimes were not social occasions at all, especially in the early years of my time at Nazareth House.

Every mealtime followed the same pattern: eat your meal, then clear the tables. We were supposed to start and finish together, but in practice, this didn't always happen. Certain foods would send my anxiety through the roof due to my sheer dislike for them.

Tapioca was one of those foods. A starchy pudding given for its iron, manganese, and fibre content, I detested its texture. To me, the tiny balls looked like small eyeballs, and I had a complete aversion to both the taste and texture.

On one occasion, time was ticking by, and I knew I had to finish it, but I just couldn't. I kept gagging with every attempted mouthful. Out of the corner of my eye, I saw most of the tables had been cleared. My eyes fixed in front of me as I tried to concentrate on the task at hand. Fear swept through me as I saw the particular sister approaching, not with encouragement but with anger, shouting at me for keeping everyone behind. She grabbed my hair, pulling my head back, and started to force-feed me spoonfuls of tapioca. This only made things worse, as each attempt made me gag more. She forced another spoonful in, and I vomited all over myself. Sweat poured down my face as fear coursed through my body amid her torrent of abuse. Her anger intensified as she swung me by my hair, trying to slap me.

I had witnessed this practice many times with other children. The nuns' response to children refusing to eat was always the same.

Looking back, I feel their force-feeding practices stemmed from sheer anger and frustration rather than any concern for nutrition. They were obsessed with routine and time. It was a dreadful, barbaric, and inhumane practice. I'm sure it complicated my relationship with food as an adult, leading to bouts of bulimia.

The bright dining room windows, which should have brought warmth and comfort, became symbols of my dread. The stark contrast between the sunlight streaming in and the harsh, oppressive environment inside only heightened the sense of confinement and control. The ritual of setting the tables, the silence enforced by the nuns, and the rigid routine turned what should have been a nourishing experience into a nightmare.

The psychological impact of these mealtimes was profound. The combination of physical abuse, verbal humiliation, and the constant threat of punishment created an atmosphere of fear and anxiety that permeated every aspect of our lives. As children, we were stripped of our dignity and autonomy, forced into submission by those who were supposed to care for us.

These experiences left lasting scars, both physical and emotional. The trauma of force-feeding, the humiliation of public punishment, and the constant fear of reprisal shaped my relationship with food and authority. Even now, as an adult, the memories of those mealtimes haunt me, a reminder of the cruelty I endured and the resilience I developed to survive.

CHAPTER 7:

PUNISHMENT

Punishment was a daily routine for many children. I remember one particular occasion when I was queuing up at mealtime. Although we all knew we weren't allowed to talk, some children would whisper, thinking no one would hear. Suddenly, I heard a nun shout, "Silence, Taylor!"

I knew I hadn't been talking or even whispering, and I pleaded my innocence. I knew if she thought it was me, I'd be punished. After the routine of tidying up, I heard my surname called, instructing me to wait outside the dining room. Using our surnames was common practice; it wasn't until the early seventies that our first names started to be used.

I had already figured out that I was going to be punished for talking back. I ate in the usual silence, filled with dread at what was to come. I waited nervously outside the dining room as instructed. Soon, I was dragged by the ear to the bathroom, where there was a row of sinks. The nun grabbed a piece of carbolic disinfecting soap, dark brownish in colour. Distressing as it was, I knew what she was about to do but could do nothing to stop it. She forced the piece of soap into my mouth, shouting, "You little liar."

I pleaded my innocence but to no avail. This horrific practice caused acute distress. The soap made you froth at the mouth, which led to choking and vomiting, followed by an upset stomach for days. It was an extremely unpleasant and inhumane experience.

Another frequent punishment for general misbehaviour was kneeling down with your hands above your head for hours. This caused exhaustion, anxiety, and fatigue. If you moved and a nun caught you, you were given a slap. The psychological damage from these punishments is sadly irreparable, no matter how much time has passed.

The use of a stick was common, especially by one particular nun. If you didn't sing well in the choir, you were lined up and received two whacks on the hand. The anticipation and fear as you waited your turn filled you with dread. The sound of the stick hitting the palm of your hand and the painful stinging sensation was unbearable. I would rush to a sink to run cold water over my hand to ease the pain.

These experiences left deep scars. The constant fear and anxiety became a part of everyday life. Each punishment reinforced a sense of worthlessness and fear, shaping our perceptions of authority and discipline. The harsh and punitive environment stripped away any semblance of childhood innocence, replacing it with dread and despair.

Living under such oppressive conditions, you learned to navigate the minefield of daily life, always trying to avoid the next punishment. The psychological impact was profound. The fear, humiliation, and physical pain were ever-present, leaving an indelible mark on our young minds. Despite this, we somehow found ways to cope, developing a resilience that would carry us through the darkest times.

The memories of these punishments are vivid and haunting. They serve as a reminder of the cruelty we endured and the strength we found within ourselves to survive. The journey towards healing is ongoing, but the resilience we developed in the face of such adversity remains a testament to our enduring spirit.

CHAPTER 8:

SEGREGATION

One thing I could never understand was how as an institution they could claim to have a child's best interests at heart, while clearly failing to do so. My brother and I were somewhat fortunate as we were infants and had an older sister. They had a segregation policy on arrival, females on one side and males on the other. However, infants with older siblings were an exception – including in our case - and as a consequence of this we remained with our sister who already had been there for a few years.

I witnessed many siblings arriving together, only to be separated, causing total distress. It was heartbreaking to see siblings torn apart, their cries echoing in the corridors. In modern times, this practice would be unacceptable, as we now understand the damaging impact that separating siblings has on individuals.

In the early days, my sister was with me and my brother because we were so young. Although I had my own journey and story, so did my sister, and I am aware she had a very traumatic time in Nazareth House. She did her utmost to try and protect both me and my brother, stepping in to defend us and occasionally taking a beating for us. But she couldn't be with us all the time. Later in life, she shared some of the horrific things she had endured, which came as no surprise when we were reunited forty years later, having lost contact for so long.

Like many displaced families, we had little chance of being reunited. There was no policy back then to keep families together. Instead, many families were separated, scattered across the UK and even further afield. Some siblings didn't even know they had brothers or sisters, with many ending up in places like Australia, displaced through no fault of their own. This is a dreadful indictment of a society that chose such a heartless option.

The separation of siblings added another layer of trauma to an already harsh existence. The comfort of a familiar face, a shared bond, was denied to many of us, increasing the sense of isolation and abandonment. The emotional scars of these separations ran deep, affecting our ability to trust and form relationships in the future.

My sister's presence, although limited, was a beacon of hope. She tried to shield us from the worst of the abuse, standing up for us when she could. Her bravery and love provided a sliver of comfort in a world filled with fear and pain. Her stories of endurance and resilience became a testament to the strength we all had to find within ourselves.

Reuniting with my sister after forty years brought a mixture of joy and sorrow. Joy at finding each other again, sorrow at the years lost and the shared pain we had endured separately. Her accounts of what she faced confirmed the horrors I had always suspected but never fully knew. Our reunion was bittersweet, a reminder of what we had survived and the bonds that could not be broken despite the distance and time.

The cruel policy of sibling separation left many of us feeling incomplete, constantly searching for a part of ourselves that had been torn away. The impact of this policy was profound, creating lifelong wounds that many of us still struggle to heal. It is a stark reminder of the cold and unfeeling system that prioritised order over the well-being of children.

CHAPTER 9:

FRESH AIR AND FREEDOM

Although in the early sixties Nazareth House was a place filled with fear and depression, things began to change significantly in the early seventies. I believe a major factor for this shift was the passing of some of the old guard nuns, who upheld very strict and archaic practices. Fresh ideas began to circulate about how to do things differently, and new nuns were brought in. Accountability became more prominent in the mid-seventies, and it was inevitable that things had to change.

My daily life started to improve gradually. Many of the old practices seemed to vanish, and it felt like a breath of fresh air had swept through the place. There was a collective sigh of relief, and like many, my anxieties eased with a growing sense of hope and the expectation that, maybe, just maybe, things were changing for the better.

I can't recall the exact year we first went to Tombae, but I vividly remember the day we were informed we were going on holiday. Tombae was a place I had never heard of, and we were all very excited as we had never been on a holiday before. We learned that Tombae was situated in Tomnavulin in Banffshire, with a house next to The Church of the Incarnation. We all simply referred to it as Tombae.

The thoughts running through my mind were difficult to describe; it was like an exciting new adventure was about to unfold, something I had never experienced in my short life. It was sheer escapism from the concrete jungle I had known, a world filled with cruel memories.

In the days leading up to our departure, there was a different atmosphere. The excitement was palpable and euphoric. We were given small bags containing plastic-patterned washbags with drawstrings, including soap, a flannel, toothpaste, and a toothbrush. Even receiving these personal items was a big deal to us, as we had never owned anything personally in our entire lives.

I remember the day we departed for Tombae vividly. The sun was shining, and the sky was a clear, perfect blue. It felt as though the old rules and practices that had been in place for years had disappeared overnight, although it surely took longer. We were loaded onto the bus, all cheerful and smiling with excitement. There was an air of expectancy on the bus as we looked forward to new adventures. I spent the entire journey, like many others, staring out the window, fascinated by the beautiful countryside we passed, something none of us were accustomed to.

We stopped in Huntly, a picturesque small town on the banks of the River Bogie, for a bite to eat. Then we continued our journey to Dufftown and beyond. Traveling along a country road, there were shouts of excitement when someone spotted a small white sign on the left that simply said 'Tombae,' about a mile up the road.

As we arrived and looked out of the bus windows, it felt like stepping into a different world. The sense of liberation and wonder was overwhelming, a stark contrast to the oppressive environment of Nazareth House. The countryside, with its rolling hills, lush greenery, and vibrant flowers, felt like a paradise to us.

We all got off the bus, and there stood an old church with a house next to it, surrounded by a graveyard both in front and behind, enclosed by a stone wall. Opposite the church, on the other side of the road, was a big hill covered in lush green grass with a treeline at the top.

Everywhere I looked, there was a paradise of green ferns, Scottish thistles, and an array of wildflowers. It felt like heaven. As a child, it was magical—a playground full of excitement, adventure, and possibilities. I had never experienced anything like it before, and I'm sure most of the other children felt the same euphoria I did that day.

We were immediately allowed to explore. I decided to walk up the road and spotted an old schoolhouse that had obviously been there for years, with a rusty green car parked next to it.

I spent many happy hours pretending to drive that car in a world of imagination. Wild chickens roamed freely, laying eggs in their coops. In the distant fields, sheep and cows grazed sights I had never seen before.

In the far distance, I saw a hill called the 'Bochel' in the Grampian Mountains, which I climbed on several occasions during my time in Tombae. The landscape leading to it was like a sea of purple heather, a sight to behold. For me, it was truly a magical place to be.

We all settled in very easily; it was hard not to. That first evening, we went for a walk into the countryside. As I walked along the road, I was overwhelmed by the peace I felt, a peace I had never experienced before. It was unnerving yet wonderful.

As we made our way back, the sound of crickets filled the air as the sun set and twilight set in. A slight chill came into the air as we huddled into a small kitchen for supper before going to bed. That first evening gave me a feeling of contentment I had never known before. With all the fresh air and excitement, I soon fell asleep.

Most days, we were allowed to explore and run freely around the surrounding fields. One day, we walked to the post office in Tomnavulin, about a mile down the road from Tombae, near a distillery. I loved that walk along the summer road, giving us all a sense of freedom that was indescribable as a child. We crossed the River Livet on an old iron footbridge that led us up a winding path near the distillery, small shop, and post office.

By this time, we had all received our pocket money, handed to us individually. There was plenty to buy at the shop, including small fishing nets that most of us bought.

Behind the house at Tombae, the River Livet wound its way down towards Tamnavulin. On many bright summer days, we made our way through the abundance of green ferns, nettles, and thistles to access the water. We would cast our small fishing nets, hoping to catch minnows and tiny fish, placing them in jam jars for the duration of our holidays. This experience was far removed from what any of us could wish for.

There was always a sports day at some point, where we all took part in various races, including the classics—the sack race, egg and spoon race, and other running races. We were never bored, enjoying long walks on sunny days and nighttime swims in the River Livet by the old footbridge across to Tomnavulin.

At this particular time in my life, it was difficult to comprehend why we experienced what we did growing up in Nazareth House.

.oOo.

I visited Tombae many years later in 2021 with my sister before she passed away. I remember getting out of the car and standing on the road opposite the church, with a rush of emotions taking me back to my childhood memories in Tombae.

I quickly realised it wasn't the same as I had remembered. Although the church still stood, and I could still match some of the scenery to my memories, it wasn't the same. As a child, I had been euphoric getting off the bus on my first visit; this was very different as an adult—and I understood that. We both felt different. There just wasn't the love that we had felt all those years ago. On our drive back, we discussed our feelings and emotions of that day.

It had been a special day, and I'm grateful we had the opportunity to visit and go back in time, sharing different stories that gave us a feeling of warmth and love—reminiscing about some good times. It certainly helped in some way the healing process in the short term and recognising the pain we both had endured. Sadly, my sister passed away on June 18th, 2023, but she remains in my thoughts every day.

CHAPTER 10:
CHANGE

When I was around 14 years old, I was sitting in the living room watching TV when I heard my name being called. We had to make our way to the front parlour in the reception area. At this point, I assumed we had a visitor—not that we were accustomed to having many—so I was curious about who it could be. Once we arrived, we were introduced to a social worker who informed us that there might be a possibility for both my brother and me to be placed with a foster family in the Aberdeen area. He asked us how we felt about this.

As I recall, we both weren't initially excited. It was all a bit overwhelming after spending the last twelve years in Nazareth House. We were somewhat numb, to be honest. This was in the mid-seventies, and things were progressively changing—many of the cruel practices were disappearing, and new nuns had been brought in. Gone were the big dining rooms and dormitories; they had been scaled back to provide smaller units with no more than eight children in each.

There was a very good feeling about the changes being made. I had stopped wetting the bed, and there was a distinctly more relaxed atmosphere. The new nun who took over had a very laid-back way of doing things—whether this was deliberate or just her personality, we all embraced it. I remember not long after she arrived, around eight in the evening, she brought a few trays into the sitting room with cocoa, iced buns, toast, and fruit. We all sat in amazement that this was happening. Nevertheless, it brought smiles to many faces that evening as we settled down to watch a film. This small act gave us all a sense of normality, and things were looking up.

A few weeks passed, and I was informed that social services were visiting, bringing the parents of the family who were to be our new foster parents. We were paraded in front of them in the parlour and introduced. I didn't really know what to say—should I sound grateful or just be myself? I was very mistrusting of any adults, and they were no different. There was some small talk, and clearly, they were out to impress. By this time, I had very mixed emotions. I had been institutionally abused for the last twelve years, but more recently, things had massively improved, so my head was all over the place. I was around fourteen then.

On this particular occasion, we were invited to go for a drive as the foster parents had to do their weekly shop. We drove to a big supermarket called Fine Fare in the Bridge of Don area in Aberdeen to do their family shop. This in itself was a new experience, and to be honest, we both enjoyed it. Another few weeks passed, and we had another visit. This time, we were introduced to their four children—three boys and a girl. Pleasantries were exchanged, and we were taken to where we would be staying. The house was a three-bedroom council house, and we were informed we would be sharing with their two older boys.

It was a tight squeeze with two sets of bunk beds in one room. The house was smaller than I expected, but it even had a small back garden. Later that day, we were returned to Nazareth House. Initially, they seemed eager to foster us, although we knew very little about them. A date was finally set, and we were informed we were leaving Nazareth House.

When the day finally came, we both had mixed emotions about leaving. You would have thought we would be elated, but we weren't. It all happened so quickly, and we had so many things to adjust to. Not only did we have a new home, but we also started a new school—the same school as our foster parents' children. We didn't adjust well. Mornings were hectic, and from the outset, we felt treated differently than their own children, who were favoured most of the time. Psychologically, we were so damaged that, no matter who we were placed with, we would find it difficult to adjust and fit in.

Our foster father was very strict and was studying to be a minister in the Methodist church. There were many arguments between our foster parents, often spilling over into physical altercations. Our foster mother was most definitely a victim of domestic abuse, both physically and mentally. He would also lash out in fits of rage towards his own sons, and eventually, we were at the end of a few punches. His anger outbursts usually happened on Saturday evenings when he was writing his sermon for the Sunday service. On many occasions, he would fly into a rage just before we were about to leave for church, then an hour later, he would be preaching to a congregation about how wonderful God was and to be kind to one another. I can now reflect on the absolute hypocrisy of the man.

Yet again, we had been failed by adults. The foster placement clearly wasn't working out, even though we ended up staying there for around two years. As time progressed, I sat my O' levels, and to my complete surprise, I passed six of them. I decided that once I reached sixteen, I would join the Army.

CHAPTER 11:
THE ARMY

We had discussed joining the Army with our foster parents. Looking back, it was clear to all of us that the foster placement hadn't really worked out. For me, it was just another cycle of abuse, an abuse of power, coercion, and control—history repeating itself.

We made the necessary inquiries and scheduled an appointment at the recruiting office. After a short test, we could choose our regiments, although it depended on our scores. My brother opted for a Scottish infantry regiment, while I would train in the Junior Leaders Regiment down in the south of England. We had about six weeks before we joined and were advised to get fit by running, which I decided to do. So for six weeks, I ran every day and managed to get myself into a reasonable level of fitness.

I remember the day I departed, all packed up and ready to go, with little confidence in what the future would hold. I knew I wouldn't see my brother again for about a year.

I had a very long train journey ahead of me, filled with apprehension about what lay ahead, but also a kind of elation and euphoria that I had escaped Aberdeen and all the memories associated with living there. I think I slept for most of the journey. I had to change trains twice at different stations, which was a bit unnerving as I had never travelled outside Scotland. At sixteen, I had never travelled so far on my own.

As the train pulled into the station at my final destination, I felt a surge of apprehension. As soon as I was on the platform, I spotted a uniformed sergeant screaming and shouting at the top of his voice for us to move. I picked up my suitcase and ran like there was no tomorrow. There were a few of us who had travelled down from Scotland. Once outside the station, we boarded a four-ton army truck, climbing up the back of it as we were shouted at again. For some reason, I found this amusing as I climbed up with ease while others struggled. Once we arrived, we were escorted off the bus and paraded outside the guardroom for further instructions. Many of the young lads looked lost and bewildered, but all the shouting and bawling didn't phase me at all. I began to think I could actually enjoy this as I had already been totally institutionalised; I was used to this.

After a very long day, we settled down for the night. By now, I had worked out how I was going to cope, unlike others. We stood and pressed our uniforms for the next day. Some were good at bulling boots—a form of spit-polishing boots—while others were good at ironing. We all mucked in together, and a sense of camaraderie was already building. I had a feeling I had made the right choice to join up.

As I lay my head down that night, I briefly thought about my past. I listened to young lads crying themselves to sleep. I was fine. I packed all my emotions and feelings deep in my mind into metaphorical boxes, determined—for now anyway—to leave them there.

I seemed to adapt very quickly to the strict regime. Soon, I was running for miles and became very fit.

When we paraded in the morning, I heard the Sergeant Major shout, "Tallest to the right, shortest to the left, single rank size."

All the lads scattered to find their places. I found this quite amusing because, with no panic, I made my way to the extreme left and was always the last man on the left due to my size and stature, being the shortest in the squadron. I was then nicknamed Titch, which I took as an endearing nickname.

Make no mistake, training wasn't easy, both physically and emotionally. We were pushed to our limits, all character-building. Although my character had already been moulded, I fit in quite well with most of the lads and gained a sense of humour, which most definitely helped.

I remember during training when everyone received letters from home. I never received any letters from anyone. I made out it didn't bother me, but the reality was it did. Not that I was even expecting any form of encouragement; I hadn't made any real connections with my foster parents. They certainly weren't nurturing in nature.

I had this ability to emotionally detach myself quite easily. I'm sure I came across as quite introverted at first. I didn't really want to share any of my past with anyone. I had no time to be emotional anyway, being in a male-dominated environment where it would have been seen as a weak trait. I remained like that for many years.

I remember about ten weeks into training, we were informed that the following weekend we had time off and were allowed leave to go home. I had already made up my mind that I didn't want to return to Scotland as there was nothing there for me. One of my mates, whom I got on really well with, invited me to his parents' home for the weekend in Kent. His parents were lovely and very welcoming.

The day arrived after many months of hard training—the passing-out parade was upon us. Most lads were excited because their families had travelled from all over the UK. I received a letter—the only letter throughout my training—from my foster parents a few days earlier, informing me they were unable to attend due to the distance involved. There was no surprise for me at all.

We all passed out that day. It was a memorable occasion for me and probably the first time I allowed myself to be proud of something I had achieved. Everyone gathered for tea and sandwiches surrounded by their families. I stood rather awkwardly on my own, not knowing what to do with myself. The Sergeant Major called me over and congratulated me on passing out, making it clear that initially, I had been a target to get rid of due to my size and stature. But he said I had proved not only him but others wrong, calling me a "stubborn wee shit" and telling me I should be proud of myself. It made me feel better.

Although it was an emotional day, it was the first time I felt worthy of something and maybe, just maybe, that I could achieve in life.

My first posting was to London. The usual apprehension built up until I arrived. It wasn't long before I built up friendships and started to enjoy myself, gaining promotion along the way. I suited army life, which I'm sure would be no surprise to most. Their job was to knock you down in training and build you up again. The only difference with me was I had already had so many knocks in life that they couldn't have brought me down any lower, but they certainly built up my confidence in ways I never imagined.

The Army was where I was introduced to alcohol. I remember the first time I had around two pints. Once I hit my pillow, the room started to spin. Slowly but surely, my tolerance level to alcohol improved. Like most young men, I would get hammered at the weekends. I wasn't always happy doing so, but it helped with social situations, and in the Army, it was actively encouraged with many happy hours on Friday afternoons.

.oOo.

I spent seventeen years in the Army, gaining further promotion and spending time in London, Rheindahlen in Germany, Northern Ireland, and the Falkland Islands.

I can honestly say they were probably some of the best years of my life.

I had many opportunities in the Army. In sport, I loved running in my early career and always made the cross-country team, achieving many medals. When based in Germany, I qualified as an offshore hand and sailed from Keil to Faaborg in Denmark, then on to Sønderburg in a catamaran, a sailing boat which was quite an adventure. I also had many opportunities to abseil and canoe on adventure training throughout my time in the Army; I had little time to even think about my past, but it was well hidden by then.

I've always been fascinated by how the mind has the ability to compartmentalise the past into metaphorical boxes in the recesses of our memory. It can keep thoughts and emotions locked away for years, under control, until one day, for whatever reason, it can no longer hold them there. When this happens, it's as if the floodgates of emotion are opened, and they become all-consuming and overwhelming. In a flash, your past revisits you, sometimes with no warning, and I have learned how crippling that can be.

Writing this book has been a journey, sometimes a very painful one. I have been triggered many times in recounting my past, but there is something cathartic about putting your own words down about your own individual thoughts and feelings. It has been a way to process how my past has impacted my life. There have been occasions where I've wondered if it was worth the mental strain it has put me under. Yet, I always concluded that I wouldn't change anything at all; it has all been part of my journey, hopefully leading to healing. I believe my past holds the key to my healing. As the title "Healing Shadows" suggests, the shadows of my past, though not fully revealed, have initiated my healing process.

CHAPTER 12:
TRANSITION

In 1993, I decided to take voluntary redundancy from the Army, enticed by a fairly good financial settlement. After seven years of marriage, it felt like the right time to make a change. We were all tired of the constant moving and me being away for long periods. My wife's family lived in Belfast, so it was a no-brainer that we would settle in Northern Ireland.

We bought our first house in a seaside resort in County Down—a reasonably sized semi-detached home with a lovely garden. However, we only stayed there for nineteen months. Once I secured employment, we moved to a larger detached house. After the stress of finding a house and getting a mortgage was over, I had to think about what I would do for an ongoing career. I had never really thought about it before. Fortunately, a relative of my wife knew someone who worked in a facility for children with challenging behaviours.

I attended a brief interview, which felt more like an informal chat. It was agreed that I would start on a casual basis once my Police Enhanced Disclosure was cleared. About four weeks later, I received a call asking if I could come in at 4 PM for an evening shift.

Having never done anything like this before, I was quite nervous and didn't know what to expect. That first shift was a baptism of fire. I quickly learned that I was seen as the newbie and an obvious target for some of the kids to test boundaries. There was no formal training given. During the handover, I sat in the meeting and received specific information about each child and their day. At this time, I had no access to any files since I was only a casual worker.

Once I left the office, I could feel the tension in the air. Some of the children paced up and down the corridor as if waiting for something to happen. It seemed like an "us versus them" situation. I felt many barriers needed to be broken down, but I wondered how to do it. As they said, Rome wasn't built in a day. It took many months of just being present, listening, and observing. I didn't want to take the easy route of just being an observer; I genuinely wanted to get to know them and build solid working relationships.

I soon learned that many children looked for any chinks in the armour of staff members to test vulnerabilities. They would ask about religious backgrounds, call names, or try to find out personal details. It could be very intimidating. I realised this was part of their defence mechanism, protecting themselves from adults they perceived as controlling.

The best advice I received was to get in amongst them, so that's what I did. My past experience of being in care helped me, though I didn't realise it at the time. This wasn't going to be a walk in the park. That first day, I introduced myself to those in the corridor, telling them my name and that it was my first shift.

They looked me up and down, and one of them said, "Who gives a fuck who you are? You're all the same— full of shit."

I wasn't sure what response I was expecting, but it certainly wasn't that one. I quickly understood that these kids had been let down by the system or significant adults in their lives. They came from diverse backgrounds, including different religious backgrounds, which was significant in Northern Ireland. I would be tested many times by them, but I understood why. For most of them, trust had been broken.

I had a lot to learn. As time went on, I saw possibilities and potential for good working relationships. I felt a sense of purpose walking through the doors and could relate to many of the issues I witnessed. Many of them were very angry for various reasons. I couldn't fix them, but I could listen—really listen—to what they were saying. Many of them self-harmed, which was always difficult to witness. It was a clear cry for help.

Most employees had their own way of doing things. In the early days, I was probably seen as very black-and-white in my interactions. It was about protection, following the rules, and finding my way, which seemed to work for me. It wasn't long before I received calls asking me to come in every day. I started to enjoy what I was doing, building solid working relationships with those I looked after.

As I gained more confidence and skills, I realised I had a natural empathetic nature. I attributed this to my traumatic past, which helped me understand many of the issues I was trying to address. Many incidents I dealt with involved distress and anger. I appeared to have the ability to de-escalate situations, but it didn't happen overnight. Building trust took time, something I never had from many adults growing up, so I genuinely understood.

Many colleagues encouraged me and saw potential in me, though I didn't see it. I kept working hard, and soon I was asked to cover shifts every day. Kids like consistency—a friendly face, someone they know. They didn't like it when a new member of staff appeared.

One thing I noticed was that if you had a couple of days off, they would notice and back off when you returned, almost as if they took it personally. Naturally, they had their favourites.

Over the years, I gained more skills than I realised and managed various situations, from kids barricading themselves in rooms to self-harm, absconding, or solvent abuse. I remember one particular morning, a young boy asked to speak to me. He informed me he had wet the bed and looked completely embarrassed. This was probably the first time I realised what empathy and dignity meant. With no fuss, I reassured him it wasn't a problem and helped him change the sheets without anyone knowing. This small act of humanity helped break down barriers with this boy. On the day he left, he thanked me for "not embarrassing me." His comment resonated with me deeply, and I felt good about making a difference. Sadly, I heard a few years later that he had been involved in a car accident and had passed away at a young age.

Some situations required physically restraining kids to protect them and us. This was never pleasant. If I was involved, I took it personally, feeling like I had failed. Even though it was a last resort, it wasn't an experience anyone liked. Many kids in our units were there because of various abuses, which manifested as anger. No shift was the same; it was always different.

A few years later, I was given the opportunity to do a DIPSW—a Diploma in Social Work. Self-doubt crept in, and my confidence dipped. I was constantly reminded that I was capable, but I didn't feel academically ready. With a lot of encouragement, I decided to pursue the qualification.

CHAPTER 13:
PANDORA'S BOX

One thing I quickly realised was that my drinking had become more frequent and I was socialising more than I was used to. Later, it became a problem that crept up on me.

I suppose I never even thought about mental health or anxiety as a condition. I used to have these overwhelming feelings of being really low, which obviously affected my thoughts, feelings, and emotions. If I'm honest, I really didn't know how to manage them. My mood could literally change within seconds. One minute I could feel like the joys of spring, and the next I would feel on my knees.

There were extreme highs, but with them came extreme lows. After I left the army, I found adapting to civilian life a lot more difficult than I ever anticipated. I had much more responsibility, which I probably didn't realise at the time, and it impacted my personal life and marriage as time went on.

No one really knows what comes with marriage. Very often, we just trundle along not knowing what we are meant to be doing. It's easy to look back and reflect on the positive aspects of our marriage, but seldom on the negatives, which were numerous for me. I wasn't easy to live with, especially after I left the army. The last thing I wanted was more failure; my childhood had been a massive failure. Little did I know that my trauma was rearing its ugly head, and by this time, I hadn't made the connection.

I became very good at masking my emotions and how I was really feeling. I would turn up for a shift at work and be almost manic in my persona—quite hyper, pretending to myself that I was happy. The reality was, I wasn't—far from it. I hid it so well. I didn't allow myself to show my real self to the world. I didn't know who the real me was. Sure, I was happy that I had made something of myself, and that's the perception I wanted—or maybe needed—to give. Keeping up a persona of not having a care in the world can be very draining. My mood swings were up and down like a yo-yo.

I remember on one occasion a colleague called me into the office with a worried look on her face and asked if everything was okay.

I, of course, answered, "Yes, why?"

She went on to say how she had noticed that on many occasions when I arrived for my shifts, I was very upbeat and hyper, but sometimes my whole mood would change very quickly.

I knew deep down she was right, and I responded with the usual, "No, honestly, everything's grand," with that awful, overwhelming, anxious feeling as if the spotlight was on me. Standing there, trying my best to smile and reassure her.

Sometimes I felt like a fraud, as if I was trying to impersonate someone. I was trying to hide my mental health struggles that had been well hidden in my previous career, even though I hadn't a clue what mental health was.

I had always seen myself as very introverted, although I'm sure many people I worked with saw me as a very young and confident individual, which was far from the reality. I winged it most of the time, not wanting to let anyone down. It was all about succeeding in life, regardless of the trauma I had endured. I had never talked to anyone about what I had been through. I wasn't sure what difference it would make. Nothing could change the past, and that seemed to be my mindset.

I continued working as months became years, becoming quite skilled along the way. Thinking back, I wonder how I ever managed my mental health initially. At the time, alcohol played a major role in numbing my deep-rooted feelings about the past. I never thought about how long I could last without something giving way. I started gambling and would visit the bookies on Saturday mornings, spending significant amounts of money looking for that high, or that buzz, to fill whatever void needed filling. It was never filled, though. All I did was make the situation feel ten times worse than before I started.

As any gambler knows, when you lose, you have that awful gut feeling as if someone has stabbed you in the stomach and twisted the knife slowly. Then come the waves of emotions—guilt and shame. You not only let down your family and friends, but you also let down yourself.

You want to stop, but you keep chasing that big win, which never comes. At the time, I never knew why I was doing what I was doing. I now realise I have an addictive personality and clearly had no idea.

So, between gambling and drinking at the weekends, it was only a matter of time before things took their toll. And they did. I started taking time off because I just couldn't face going to work. Up until then, I had a fairly good attendance record, so as far as my employers were concerned, there were no real alarm bells yet. My gambling habits affected my financial affairs, which just added to my overall mental health issues and guilt towards my family.

Many times I told myself I'd cut down on drinking and stop gambling, and there were periods when that happened. Even with all this chaos in my head, I still had the ability to function. God knows how, but I did. By this time, I had gained significant experience and skills. I openly say I deserved an Oscar for hiding my mental health because I gave Oscar-winning performances in masking my true feelings and emotions.

I remember one occasion when I was discussing with a colleague how their weekend had been. We had just started a shift like most mornings, and my mood was very upbeat—too upbeat, if I'm honest. As I was standing there, giving eye contact, an overall sadness came over me. I could see them standing there in a blur, listening to their conversation but not really listening. There was no trigger, but my eyes started filling up, and my mood changed completely, and I had no control over it. It was almost like an out-of-body experience. I could see both of us standing there, with me just staring at him, the conversation ending abruptly.

I made my way to the bathroom and broke down, but I hadn't a clue why this was happening. The mask was slipping; Pandora's box was fighting to open. It's difficult to put into words when you have no control over your emotions, when they seem to come from nowhere. I saw this as a weakness and probably beat myself up about why I allowed this to happen. I had shown little emotion in my past career.

Life carried on, and I managed my mental health struggles, never really acknowledging them or realising I wasn't coping with life. I was simply putting a sticking plaster on them, thinking surely it would get better. I was right, in the short term. I had periods where things seemed okay—whatever 'okay' means—but I carried on working, and the majority of the time, I enjoyed what I was doing.

CHAPTER 14:
I MADE IT

Time was moving on, and I had been working in the same job for around eight years. Eventually, I landed a spot on the Diploma in Social Work (DIPSW) course, which was a massive achievement for me. The thought of qualifying as a Social Worker felt monumental, considering my past. However, I had reservations about whether I was academically capable of achieving it. From the outset, I put myself under a lot of pressure. Naturally, I was an overthinker, and my anxiety levels were through the roof.

I quickly found out that the social work industry had its own language and jargon. It was a struggle for me. I found myself almost having to rethink how I communicated. Maybe it was just me, but I felt strongly that communication should be simple and straightforward rather than filled with long-winded reports and jargon. Ironically, though, I had to adapt, and I did.

When I arrived on the course, it was quite daunting. There were people from all walks of life. We had to introduce ourselves and explain our work backgrounds. There were people from childcare, disability, and elderly care backgrounds, creating a good mix.

As time progressed, I found our group very warm and caring. They were all genuinely lovely people and very supportive of each other. We got to know everyone well and had many class discussions on different subjects. I seemed to thrive on these discussions, and a few people commented on how experienced I was. Like most praise, I didn't really take it on board. I didn't see myself as 'experienced,' although I had gained many skills in dealing with challenging behaviours and had become a very good listener. I was quite surprised at how many things I was already doing without realising it.

The course included many exercises and tasks to open up discussion and debate. One task, in particular, became significant in my journey. We were given a bunch of magazines and told to create a collage of pictures describing our lives. I thought this would be easy, but I found myself struggling. I had never really thought about my past at all.

I remember cutting out pictures of nuns, tanks, soldiers, a bowl of porridge, and a picture of a man's face split in two. One side of the face was smiling, and the other was dark and worried, with a caption that read, "Don't wear your mask." This resonated with me, so I included it in my collage.

After completing the task, we had to stand up and explain our collages. When it was my turn, I stood up and began to be very open and honest, not realising the emotional implications.

As I started to explain each picture, anxiety swept over me. When I reached the image of the split face, I felt my voice breaking. Suddenly, I broke down and started crying uncontrollably, unable to stop.

I was taken out of the class to gather myself. When I returned, everyone was very supportive. The tutor asked me to stay behind after class. He was empathetic and explained that images can be powerful in bringing back memories.

This was probably the first time I had thought deeply about my past. It was a milestone I will never forget.

We were down to our final paper—an eight-thousand-word essay from psychological, international, and present-day perspectives. I titled mine "Solvent Abuse: A Complex Issue for Young People." It took me many hours to write, and I struggled with my confidence. I had very little self-belief, which I still struggle with today.

To my astonishment, my final paper passed. I remember the morning I received the letter informing me I had passed. After the ceremony, I would be a Qualified Social Worker. A wealth of emotion came over me knowing I had achieved what I set out to do, despite my mental health struggles being at their peak.

Somehow, I managed to mask everything I was going through.

The resilience in me seemed to be a common occurrence. I had so much to give, constantly up against overwhelming doubts. But somehow, I dug deep and managed to achieve my goal.

Our graduation ceremony took place at The King's Hall Conference Centre in Belfast. Even as I took my place among all the other graduates, I couldn't believe it. It was almost as if I wasn't good enough or maybe they had made a mistake.

The place was packed, and my anxiety was through the roof with a multitude of emotions running through my mind. I wasn't handling it well at all. I felt myself welling up inside, wanting to break down and cry. Floods of memories from my past decided to visit me that day.

I pictured that small boy riding a red tricycle around a concrete playground, with no memory of a mother or father, but memories of childhood abuse. As I sat there, almost contemplating giving myself a pat on the back or a well-done, a friend asked, "Are you ok?"

I replied, "I'm fine," those infamous words often used to hide the truth.

As I walked up to be presented with my certificate, I fought back my emotions, tears in my eyes, biting my lip to hold back the flood of feelings. I bit so hard that my lip was bleeding when I returned to my seat.

Many people congratulated me that day, not knowing the emotions I was going through. I had made it—whatever that meant. I was soon to find out what mental health struggles were really about.

CHAPTER 15:

CLOUDS LOOMING

After I qualified, I continued in the same employment but with much more responsibility and accountability. I hadn't realised how emotionally draining the course had been. After the euphoria of qualifying, I came down with a bang from the massive high I had been on. My marriage had come to an end, and everything began to get on top of me. I became an emotional wreck, my gambling addiction increased, and I really felt very low. Reflecting back, I now realise that I was more likely than not spiralling into a deep depression, but I hadn't put a name to it.

It was only a matter of time before I had to take sick leave because I had no regulation regarding my moods whatsoever. I was a total mess, breaking down quite often. Tears would just drip down my face at the slightest thing. My concentration levels were zero, with my anxiety through the roof.

I remember sitting in my GP's surgery, breaking down, trying to make sense of what was going on. I had felt low at times, but never like this. It was almost like a black cloud hovering over my head twenty-four hours a day. I had no sense of reality anymore. Everything in my life was out of control. At the time, all I felt was a massive failure to everyone—my family, my friends, and my colleagues.

I started to have panic attacks, not knowing what they even were. I remember leaving a bookies after just losing a significant amount of money, then out of nowhere my heartbeat started racing a million miles an hour. Then I got chest pains and a feeling of drowning in absolute fear. My anxiety levels were so high I could hardly breathe. This was the first of many panic attacks I would experience in the coming months.

I had moved into rental accommodation by this time and the realisation that I was experiencing very dark and low moods set in. I felt incredibly lonely and would switch off my phone for days, keeping the curtains closed to escape from the outside world. I always felt safest not moving from my bed; not having to communicate with anyone allowed me to wrap my loneliness around me like a safety blanket. I started having night terrors from my past, waking up in cold sweats, constantly dreaming about everything that had happened thirty-odd years earlier. I couldn't understand it. Why now?

I had these overwhelming feelings of guilt and shame too. One particular morning, I woke and realised I had wet the bed after a particularly bad dream. It was clear to me that my past had decided to make a visit.

My life seemed pointless, or at least that's how I felt. I had lost everything. I started drinking most days. I wasn't stupid—I knew alcohol was a depressant—but at the time, it numbed the pain. I hadn't spoken to my kids in a while, which I felt deeply ashamed of. I loved them dearly and often wondered why I was behaving the way I was, but in all honesty, I was ashamed.

My self-esteem was at an all-time low. I was going through a cycle of just abusing my body and mind. I really didn't know who I was anymore.

Part of me felt fake. How could I be a qualified social worker and be in the state I was in? I genuinely didn't know how to feel anymore. I was numb about life.

All my insecurities seemed to come back, and I had zero confidence in myself or my future—if I had any. I would often talk myself into thinking I could bounce back, but it didn't last very long.

My days became very long, and I seemed to be on a road to self-destruct. I spent many hours in bed feeling totally lost and overwhelmed by absolutely everything. I was crippled with shame, guilt, and anxiety. By this time, my GP had told me I was suffering from anxiety and depression. This was probably the first time I had even thought about the word, let alone its symptoms.

I started using the expression "dark clouds looming" to describe how I could feel myself slipping into depression. Unfortunately, it could be triggered very easily. Depression from then on seemed to be a never-ending battle. It had most definitely isolated me and given me that feeling that there was 'no way out.'

I thought that no one would understand as it's very complex to explain to anyone, even today. There is such a stigma when it comes to mental health and the struggles we go through. Even now, I feel embarrassed talking about it—that feeling of being so low that even though you want to crawl out of the black hole you're in, you just can't.

I often felt I just didn't want to be in this world. It was so overwhelmingly painful. All I wanted was to get off the black roller coaster of emotions. It wasn't for lack of trying. I tried everything, even thinking that running away could improve things. Obviously, this isn't true as mental health travels with you—so there is no escape.

CHAPTER 16:
DARK PLACES

Around Autumn 2005, I remember one particularly difficult week when everything felt like a major struggle. If I wasn't in bed, I was out drinking. That weekend had been particularly bad. I was extremely hungover, lying in bed and contemplating the meaning of life. It was around 11am, and I had just woken up, my mind racing a million miles an hour, trying to figure out how I had gotten myself into this mess. I felt so alone and lost, with an overwhelming sense of sadness and a desperate longing for someone to take the pain away. Yet, I couldn't ask for help. I cried incessantly that morning until I had no more tears to give. It was a very gloomy day, matching my mood perfectly. I felt totally isolated and needed to get out. Again, I felt that intense sense of guilt and shame for putting my family through this whole episode of my life, but at the same time, I had absolutely no control over my feelings, emotions, or actions.

Sceptics will always say you have choices in life, which is true to a point. But when you are so mentally unstable that those choices are removed because you are in no fit state to make any right logical choice, it can be crippling. I felt very numb that day. I didn't bother eating, although I hadn't eaten in days. When I experienced dark days, I always had an intense urge to run away or at least get away from my immediate surroundings. On this particular day, I decided to travel into Belfast. I booked a room at the infamous Europa Hotel even though I was extremely hungover. I was definitely having an ongoing battle with my demons.

I knew it wasn't a good idea for me to go drinking again, as it would only exacerbate my feelings. But I just couldn't stop myself. I travelled to Belfast and booked into the hotel. To this day, I still have no idea why I booked a hotel. Maybe it was to relieve myself of the familiarity of where I had been, which was mostly my bed or the pub. All I knew was that I intended to go on a pub crawl. I crossed over the road and walked into a pub, ironically called The Beaten Docket. I wasn't in the pub long after I had booked into the hotel, and of course, there was a bookies around the corner—how convenient!

By mid-afternoon, I had pressed my self-destruct button yet again. I knew that day wouldn't end well, and my predictions were right. Once more, I had gambled a significant amount of money and was highly intoxicated. I moved on to the Crown Bar a few hundred yards away. Although extremely drunk, I still had the ability to continue drinking. For a period of time, I just watched people, observed them, and wondered what type of life all these different characters I came across had.

It demonstrates that no one knows what anyone is going through. As a society, we are oblivious to how others are feeling at any particular time. We are all very good at masking those inner deep thoughts. The laughter and conversations soon dissipated, and I experienced an overwhelming feeling of sadness and helplessness. Even earlier, when I had gained Dutch courage to talk to complete strangers, it was all out of politeness. Inside, I was crippled with pain as I made my way to the next bar for my next Jack Daniels and Coke.

I had a female friend in Scotland whom I had been messaging throughout the day. I never really told her how I was feeling; suffice to say, she had raised her concerns by reading between the lines of my messages, even though I pretty much ignored her replies. In my head, I had gone beyond any help. There appeared to be no way out of the shit life I had recently created for myself.

As I moved from pub to pub, my conversations became less frequent, and I was drinking more and more to the point where I was sitting on my own, with tears running down my cheeks, feeling a total sense of failure in life. I had been drinking for around eight hours, and by now, I was an emotional mess. I had no logical thinking at all. I just remember thinking that I had enough and couldn't take anymore. Everyone would be better off without me because the emotional pain I was experiencing was indescribable. I felt a burden to everyone. For the first time, I felt I no longer wanted to be here anymore, and everyone would be much better off without me. Clearly, the alcohol didn't help and just made things worse.

For some unknown reason that day, I decided I was going to jump off a bridge—in fact, Queens Bridge in Belfast. It wasn't far from where I was. I have no idea why a bridge even came into my head. I started walking, making my way up Chichester Street and onto Victoria Street, stopping many times to sit on the curb, almost as if I was trying to delay what I had decided to do. I continued on my way to the bridge in a very distressed state. I decided to phone my friend on the way, clearly in a highly emotional state and crying for help or at least someone to listen to my pain. I arrived at Queens Bridge, walking on the pavement with a multitude of feelings. It was almost like an out-of-body experience, as if I was watching myself climb up onto the edge of the bridge. I had already hung up on my friend. I didn't know what else to say. By this time, I was on the edge of the bridge, contemplating jumping. My phone kept ringing, and once more, I answered it. My friend was trying to calm me down and communicate that there were alternatives. By this time, I was full of desperation, fear, and sadness. I was paralysed with all these emotions and, at that particular time, sadly felt I wanted to end my life. I wasn't thinking rationally. I had been through fight or flight mode. I never considered the consequences of my impending actions, what I would be leaving behind, or the devastation it would cause. All I was thinking was that I had to end the pain I was feeling. I had failed. I was a failure. Thoughts of my traumatic childhood came rushing back into my mind. That feeling of never being good enough was so overwhelming. All I could think was that I tried—I really did try—but it wasn't good enough.

I sat on the edge of the bridge, pouring my heart out, which seemed like forever. Distraught, my friend had kept me talking for a significant time and had managed, somehow, with another friend, to get through to the Police in Belfast. I wasn't really aware of anything around me at all. I hadn't heard anyone or seen anyone pass by, except for the occasional car headlights, as it was in the early hours by this time. But ironically, the odd car that did pass never stopped. Out of the blue, I saw headlights, but they didn't really impact me. Then, all of a sudden, two figures seemed to appear from nowhere in all-black uniforms. One of them spoke my first name and started a conversation. Then, without warning, the other policeman lunged forward and grabbed me around the waist, pulling me away from the edge of the bridge. It happened very quickly. Once I realised what had just happened, I broke down hysterically. To this day, I don't know if it was through relief or anger, but looking back, it was most certainly relief and gratitude.

I was then taken to the Royal Hospital to be assessed by the psychiatric team.

CHAPTER 17:

HOSPITAL ADMISSION

I remember waking up in A&E, initially not really knowing where I was. I was fully clothed and clearly totally hungover. Once I had gathered my thoughts, the flashbacks from the night before started to come into my mind. I lay there with tears running down my face, feeling very distressed.

I lay there for a considerable time, wondering what was going to happen. I felt full of guilt and shame, and all the negative thoughts I had about myself came rushing back from the day before. Around 8:30 in the morning, a nurse came to see me, explaining what would happen next and asking how I was feeling.

Of course, I replied, "I'm fine, just hungover." She explained that I would be seen by the psychiatric team for an assessment. I had at least a couple of hours to gather my thoughts, even though my anxiety was through the roof. Lying on that bed in A&E gave me far too much time to think. My mind was constantly racing as to what I would say to them. All I knew was that I needed to get out of there.

I did contemplate just walking out, but a part of me wanted to talk to someone, and another part didn't. I was confused; my mind was definitely not thinking straight. The longer I waited, the more anxious I felt. I remember pacing up and down in that confined space. A nurse was passing, and I spoke with her. She then got clearance to give me some medication to help me calm down.

I had already worked out what I would say to the psychiatric team. When they arrived, I went into autopilot, answering their questions. Did I have suicidal thoughts today? Did I feel I would make another attempt to take my life? I obviously said no, because, at that moment, I had no thoughts. Like most people with mental health struggles, I was very good at masking my real feelings. After a significant time, I had convinced them that I was okay and that the previous day's events were caused by alcohol.

It was agreed that I would be given support by my local mental health team. To my astonishment, I was discharged from the hospital later that day. Nothing had really changed; I had just managed, as I always had, to minimise my real feelings. I was given a number for my local mental health team, and they would set up an appointment.

I left the hospital thinking, what have I done? I really was an emotional mess. I made my way home and lay in bed for most of the afternoon. Later that evening, I decided to get a bath. I don't remember much more, other than lying in the bath. I think I ended up having some sort of panic attack. I had this total feeling of emotional pain that, at that moment, I hated myself. I needed somehow to ease that pain as it was indescribable.

At that moment, from what I can remember, I felt totally disconnected from myself and everything around me. Almost in a trance-like state, I started to cut one of my legs with a razor blade. The water turned a deep red in no time. At that particular moment, it seemed to ease my pain. It felt like a total cry for help.

I eventually snapped out of that horrendous feeling and rang the mental health team, who arrived within the hour. I sat in the corner of my front room in a very distressed state. I was then admitted to a local psychiatric ward.

Once I was admitted, I had a full assessment done a few days later. Although I was very numb and medicated, I still seemed to dissociate myself from everything around me. From my recollection, I remember just staying in bed, not wanting to move for anything. I didn't eat for the first few days.

By the third day, I didn't feel as spaced out. The nurses were very proactive in trying to instil a routine of getting up in the morning and washing, then taking breakfast. My mood was very flat. I didn't really know how to articulate how I was feeling. I had a few meetings with various professionals. Initially, they had stated I was suffering from reactive depression, a type of adjustment disorder. I have had a few diagnoses made throughout my life, but this was the first. I believe they are all linked in some way.

As time went on, life in a psychiatric ward became very routine, and if I'm honest, nothing had really changed apart from me being kept safe for my own good. My head was still a mess. I got used to the sessions I had with the staff on the ward. It was good to offload and take time out of the roller coaster of emotions I had been on. Although I still had the ability to mask how I was really feeling, it had become a trait of mine. Admitting how I was feeling would be too overwhelming regarding the shame and guilt I felt inside.

I remember sitting in a meeting about a possible discharge, and I was asked the question, "How do you feel about being discharged into the community with support from the mental health team?" It then dawned on me that I wasn't ready to return to my reality. It was too soon, and I voiced how I felt. It was then explained to me that due to a shortage of beds, I would be discharged the following day. I had been there for two weeks.

The night before I was discharged, I became increasingly anxious, with my anxiety going off the scale. I knew I wasn't ready, but it was happening. After breakfast the following day, I went through the discharge process and was discharged just after lunch.

I remember walking through the car park with a feeling of not wanting to be in my reality. The further I walked, the more anxious I became. My breathing became more rapid, and I could feel my heart thumping through my chest. A total feeling of dread came over me. All I wanted to do was run away.

The more anxious I became, the more stressed I became. I started running, making my way home. As I was running, images flashed in front of my eyes: the bridge, my children, me as a child, the hospital, and many more. It was almost like a camera shutter clicking over images at high speed.

In a very distressed state, I arrived home and felt this overwhelming urge to run away—to the point I made my way to the airport and got the next flight out—to Edinburgh, by sheer coincidence, but ironically, my birthplace.

I was dissociating from the world, feeling lost and scared. Midway through the flight, I acted out as if nothing untoward had happened over the last few hours. It wasn't until I landed that my mind kicked in to what I had just done.

I needed somewhere to go, and I managed to book a hotel in the west end of Edinburgh. Once in my hotel, I felt mentally drained and fell asleep.

I woke up a few times, this time having flashbacks about my childhood, which I had never talked to anyone about before. My mind appeared to be playing tricks on me. I had always managed to suppress any feelings and emotions before, but not this time. As much as I tried to put them back in the box I had created deep in the dark recesses of my mind, it wasn't happening.

I became quite manic about things. I decided to go out to a pub on Rose Street in Edinburgh, which wasn't far. It was déjà vu again - drowning my feelings in alcohol. I had definitely lost control and any sense of identity.

By late afternoon, I was drunk again, and those feelings of betrayal, guilt, and shame were back with a vengeance. In my head, everyone would be much better off without me. I had become such a burden and failure that I couldn't think straight. I walked to four or five different chemists, buying up paracetamol. Returning to the hotel, I made my way to my room. By this time, I wanted someone to listen to my pain. I had taken quite a few painkillers. I felt no one would understand.

In a distressed state, I ended up phoning the Samaritans in the early morning hours. The next thing I remember was a paramedic over me, trying to wake me up. I was admitted to The Royal Edinburgh Hospital psychiatric ward, where I remained for around four weeks. I was then eventually returned to Northern Ireland under escort and admitted to a psychiatric ward for a further two weeks. I had a complete mental health breakdown.

I often think back to what triggers someone to go through this and have come to the conclusion that it is a multitude of factors, and everyone is different. I had never heard of the phrase 'suicide ideation' before. There are two kinds, 'passive' and 'active'. I believe, for me personally, I've had both, particularly at that time of my life.

Sadly, I felt the way I did, genuinely thinking there was no other way out of my emotional pain and trauma. The mind is very complex and can trick you into all sorts of emotions. It's having the ability to understand what's going on that probably helped me in the end.

CHAPTER 18:
LIGHT AT THE END OF THE
TUNNEL

After I was discharged from the hospital, I continued seeing the mental health team. I had already decided to resign from my post as a social worker—I felt like an imposter, riddled with guilt and shame about my mental health. At that time, mental health had a massive stigma attached to it. It would be many years before society got to where we are today, first accepting that it exists and second, not being judged for it.

Although I was relatively stable, I felt an overwhelming need to get away. In my manic state, I decided to move back to Scotland, unable to face anyone, including family, friends, and colleagues. This was a decision I would live to regret later in life.

When I moved back, it felt as if I had been away for a lifetime. I missed my children terribly, but I had this ability to emotionally detach from my reality. This was obviously a coping mechanism for me, but not a healthy one. I remember my youngest child, around eleven or twelve, coming over to see me for a weekend.

Just before she left, she asked, "Daddy, will you come home?" She broke down, and we both cried. It was such a very emotional moment that I will never forget. This was the first time I truly realised the emotional impact my absence had caused my children. To this day, I still feel so guilty for not recognising the damage I had done, particularly to my youngest. I will forever feel riddled with guilt. I promised her I would return home within a couple of months, which I did.

Even though I knew it was the right thing to do, I also recognised that it wouldn't be easy. Something had clicked within me; I didn't want to feel the way I did anymore. It was mentally and physically draining me. I returned to my GP and got back on track with different medication and started seeing a psychiatrist weekly. As the months went by, I gained some confidence, found somewhere to live, and got a job, although not in social care.

I began to rebuild some bridges with people and felt less guilty and shameful about my mental health, although I always felt as if I was being judged. I never wanted to feel the way I did. I had clearly had some mental health breakdowns over the years, not realising I had opened up a minefield of emotions and feelings that would come to haunt me in my older years. However, it did help me understand my mental health much more.

From then on, I was fairly content with life. It wasn't perfect by any means. It took a very long time to build friendships and relationships. I was probably too open about my past to many people. Some were judgmental and didn't really understand, while others were empathetic. Unfortunately, once you open that box around your past, it never really leaves you. It becomes part of you, and all your insecurities you managed to hide throughout your lifetime come to the fore like never before. I still managed to mask how I really felt with friends and family, almost as if I didn't allow myself to feel the way I did. I tried so hard to keep my true feelings away from many people because it just wasn't talked about. Looking back, the stigma around mental health was as prominent as ever. Some people just had the attitude of "pull your socks up and get on with it," and even though I struggled most of the time, that's exactly what I did.

I was a people pleaser and never really knew why, let alone that it was related to childhood trauma. I always seemed to prioritise others' needs over my own. I learned very late in life that people-pleasing behaviour actually stems from a massive fear of rejection. Most people who go through this have low self-esteem linked to childhood trauma. When they struggle, they experience intensified feelings of anxiety and stress when their individual perception of conflict or disapproval is at their expense. I always wondered why I never had the ability to say no. This trait, unfortunately, stayed with me, even though it's hard to shift. I try each day.

Life continued with me, trying as best I could to manage my mental health. I made new friends and mixed in different circles. I fell into that mode of appearing self-assertive and a reasonably confident person, which was so far from the truth. I had many struggles with my anxieties but still had the ability to mask them, which I did for a significant number of years. I just got on with life, and it appeared as if I had managed to tame the lion regarding my mental health. It was always there, though. I hid my down days well from the world because I felt that I had been given another chance at life and didn't want to be seen as a disappointment. I suppressed many of those feelings. Although not as prominent as they had been, I constantly got reminders that they had never really gone anywhere at all. They had been parked up, almost as if they were just waiting in the wings for another crisis to come along and for them to become active once more.

CHAPTER 19:

INQUIRY

In the summer of 2017, I attended my nephew's wedding in Aberdeen. This year was significant because I finally met many family members, including my sister and brothers, some of whom I hadn't seen for forty years, and a brother I had never met. After some research on social media, I managed to find them. Following the wedding, I decided to venture into Aberdeen with lifelong friends of my sister, to get a coffee and some fresh air. Walking up Union Street in Aberdeen, many childhood memories came flooding back.

We found a coffee house and settled in. My sister's friend mentioned that an inquiry had been set up by the Scottish Government to look into historical abuse within the residential care system in Scotland, dating back to the fifties. She showed me an online article with an email address inviting anyone who had been in any residential establishment during those times to come forward and make a statement.

Reading that article gave me a lot to think about. I decided to sit on it for a few months, unsure of the personal implications and how it might impact me. After many discussions with different people, I decided to submit a request to give a statement to the inquiry. I emailed them and received a prompt response detailing the next steps. This was followed by the first of many phone calls with the inquiry team. I was assigned a key worker who was with me every step of the way.

Once certain arrangements were made, I was informed that three people from the inquiry team would fly to Belfast to take my statement. A conference room was booked in the Wellington Park Hotel in South Belfast, and I was allowed to have someone with me for support. The night before, I didn't sleep a wink, tossing and turning, wondering if this was the right thing to do. The morning of the meeting, I drove to the hotel, filled with mixed emotions—euphoria and anxiety.

Upon arrival, I was introduced to the three people present. They explained that one would ask questions, another would record my statement, and the third was my support worker from the inquiry. From the outset, they were patient, kind, and empathetic, always allowing me to stop when needed. Giving my statement was emotionally overwhelming; I became visibly distressed at times, even though I knew it might be distressing. I was lucky enough to have a friend, Aggy, who supported me throughout the process and always seemed to understand what I was going on throughout many years.

The statement-taking process lasted most of the day, with a break for lunch. It was a long and mentally draining day, more than I had anticipated. Once the statement was completed, they flew back to Edinburgh. About two weeks later, they returned to Belfast, allowing me to review and make changes to my statement. Everything was accurate, and I signed it. I was informed that a percentage of those giving statements might be invited to give evidence at the inquiry, but it was up to the individual to agree.

A few months passed, and I wasn't doing great. In the interim, I started a civil case to secure compensation for the childhood trauma I had endured, understanding that no amount of money could ever truly compensate for the abuse.

I remember thinking when the case was settled a few years later, that was the end of it … until a friend, Karen, reminded me one evening that this was just the beginning and it was actually far from over. She was right, it was just the start of an emotional roller coaster that would impact my mental health in a big way.

So, all those ideas I had about closure after the court case sadly went out of the window. The whole process had opened deep wounds and it was becoming obvious my past had come back to haunt me.

I received a call from the inquiry team, inviting me to appear at the inquiry to give evidence. They reassured me that I could change my mind up until the day I was scheduled to appear. I asked for some time to think about it, which led to panic attacks, sleepless nights, and flashbacks, turning my life into a nightmare of emotions.

Eventually, I decided to appear and tell my story despite the anxiety and doubts. It was a few more weeks before I knew when I would appear. I wanted to write and read a statement to the inquiry, a task that took me nine hours as I kept rewriting. Eventually, I felt satisfied with what I had written—a heartfelt statement representing not only my experiences but also those of others who had been psychologically damaged by the care system.

I received all the details of my appearance at the inquiry. Two people accompanied me for support— Agnes and Sharon, who were more like family than friends. We arrived in Edinburgh the day before, and my anxiety was constantly building. The inquiry accommodated us in The Hilton Hotel, not far from Mint House where the inquiry was held. The night before, we had a drink to settle my nerves, laughing and crying, with my friends constantly encouraging me and reminding me of the importance of what I was about to do.

The next day, we got up early. I was suited and booted, and we had breakfast. Not much was said, as they could see how nervous I was. My support worker arrived at the hotel and escorted us to Mint House. Agnes and Sharon took their seats assigned to the public, while I was briefed on the hearing room and who would be present. There were seats for the press, lawyers, council to the inquiry, legal representatives, and stenographers recording everything. I met with the QC who would ask me questions, and he tried to put me at ease, but my adrenaline was pumping.

I was called forward and walked into a room full of people. It was one of the most daunting experiences of my life. Lady Smith, the Inquiry chair, introduced herself and did her utmost to make me feel at ease. Queens Counsel Colin Macaulay went through my statement for the next few hours, asking many questions. I bit my tongue, holding back overwhelming emotions.

After a brief break, we resumed. Standing there, memories overwhelmed me, and I broke down on the stand, crying inconsolably. The inquiry acknowledged my distress and allowed me several opportunities to compose myself. Towards the end, the QC, Mr Macaulay, informed the Inquiry Chair, Lady Smith, that I wished to read a statement, which I did.

By this time, my anxiety levels were through the roof, but I was determined to read it. It felt euphoric standing there, explaining how my traumatic childhood had damaged me throughout my adult life. It was a powerful moment, and I broke down again, but I needed to say what I had wanted to for so many years. It was crucial to let people know how I felt and to expose the failures in the Scottish care system of the past. I needed them to understand that those involved had to take responsibility for these failings.

As before, I had to catch my breath, navigating the wealth of emotions running through my mind. I occasionally looked up, feeling all eyes on me. It was nerve-wracking. There were times I had to refocus and concentrate on reading my statement because when I lifted my head, everything seemed to blur.

It's difficult to describe how it felt in that moment. Although the process was triggering, painful, and distressing, I wouldn't change it, despite having doubts since appearing in the Inquiry, particularly as I have struggled with my mental health. Once you commit to something like that, there's no turning back after it's done.

Reading my statement was overwhelming and distressing at times, but there was a sense of pride within me, a resilience and determination to get through it all and ensure those with a duty of care admitted their failures. They needed to accept their responsibility for the psychological damage, hurt, and pain they inflicted on children.

I remember when I finally finished, Lady Smith turned to me and said, 'Your words will not go unheard. You are free to leave. Thank you.' It was such a powerful thing to say.

After the proceedings, in a side room, QC Colin Macaulay came in and said, 'Your statement was very powerful; you could hear a pin drop. Well done!' Somehow, I had managed to get through it all.

Months later, I received a copy of the damning report on Nazareth House from the Scottish Abuse Inquiry, which included Aberdeen. It concluded that children were abused in various ways, including physical, emotional, and sexual abuse. It detailed humiliation and a punitive regime for bed-wetting and force-feeding.

I sat down and read the report the morning it arrived - my mind racing a million miles an hour. The conclusions were based on many hundreds of statements. As I started reading it again, tears began running down my face, and I felt a torrent of emotions, just as I'm sure other survivors did when they read the report.

It's difficult to describe what I felt. There was an immense sense of relief that we had been listened to – but with that came overwhelming sadness. So many lives had been destroyed, and the majority of our childhoods had been stolen from us.

I am a survivor of institutionalised historical abuse, and despite the many challenges I have faced, there is a deep-rooted resilience in me and many others who have found ways to cope, although the scars of our childhood trauma never leave us.

What I probably didn't realise at the time was how triggering it all had been, and it had a massive impact on my mental health, much more than I had anticipated. However, it was part of my survival journey.

CHAPTER 20:

REVISITING

On Monday the 11th March 2024, I decided to go back to Aberdeen to revisit the home where I was brought up as a child. After discussing it with my support coordinator from Future Pathways, an organisation set up by the Scottish Government to support survivors of abuse within the Scottish Care System, we agreed a visit would take place. We considered how it might impact me emotionally and, on balance, decided it would be a positive thing to do. Like the Scottish Abuse Inquiry, it was something I felt I needed to face.

Mother's Day fell just before my departure, stirring up a mix of emotions. Sadly, I never got to meet my mother before she passed away. Sometimes I wonder if I should have made more of an effort to find her. It's a question I'll probably never be able to answer. What I will say is I have no animosity towards my mother; if anything, I feel empathetic towards her, as she clearly struggled in life. I'd be lying if I said I didn't wish things had been different, but sadly, it wasn't meant to be. In times of crisis over the years, I have had anger within me, asking what if things had been different. However, I believe everything happens for a reason.

I knew I would be very apprehensive about making that journey, as it had been forty-nine years since I left the place. I wondered what emotions it would evoke within me. I remember sitting in Belfast City Airport on the 11th of March 2024, questioning if I was doing the right thing. I was full of anxiety and trepidation, waiting for the gate number to be announced on the departure board. Like most people at airports, I watched others, wondering where they were going. Some were clearly going on holiday, young ones hitting the drink at 10am, looking excited to get away. Others were on business trips, and there I was, about to revisit the place where I had endured so many difficult times. I was on a personal journey to look back at my childhood years in the city where I was raised. I had always said I'd like to stand outside the gates of my upbringing and say to myself, "You may have ruined my childhood years, but I survived, and here I am to tell my story."

There is something very powerful in realising and acknowledging that you are a survivor of childhood abuse. Contrary to what people expect, there is a resilience and strength of character in you that comes from within and is deeply rooted. I have been knocked down both physically and mentally so many times in my life, yet somehow, I keep getting back up. I don't have the answers as to why I do, but upon reflection, it's almost like you are saying to that establishment, "You may have won many battles in knocking me down, but you did not win the war." Well, that's the analogy I have come up with, and that sits fine with me.

Sadly, not all children who went through the Scottish Care System survive. Many end up in the judicial system with very little support in trying to navigate this thing we call life. I'm the lucky one, and although I have accepted that I will always struggle with my mental health, I have developed coping mechanisms to help me in difficult times of crisis. It's not easy, but I chose life with all its roller coaster of emotions, and I am very proud of that fact.

I landed in Aberdeen late in the morning, earlier than anticipated, and my anxiety levels were pretty high. My palms were sweaty, and I felt a deep apprehension as I walked through arrivals, anxiously looking for the carousel number to collect my luggage. My mind was racing, and my heartbeat was pounding. I felt like I was about to have a panic attack but managed to avoid it by fixating on something completely different, a ploy I have often used to redirect my thoughts and avoid panic attacks with some success.

I had been to Aberdeen airport previously. Most airports look pretty much the same, full of overpriced shops and food outlets, Aberdeen being no different. I collected my luggage and made my way outside to take a taxi to my hotel. Initially, I didn't really notice my surroundings during the journey, possibly because I was deep in thought. There was little conversation between me and the driver, a silence that on this occasion didn't need to be filled. Aberdeen was very foggy and rainy, dull to say the least. If I'm honest, it looked very depressing.

Once I arrived at my hotel, I settled in. I was tired, having been awake since 5am, and no surprise, I hadn't slept well the night before. Unfortunately, insomnia comes with the territory. Nonetheless, I decided to take a walk to find somewhere to have lunch. I came across The Archibald Simpson and had a bite to eat and a pint, giving myself time to adjust to where I was and the opportunity to relax and contemplate what the next day would bring. I decided to walk up Union Street, much of which was pedestrianised. I had walked up that street many times as a child. Many shops had closed down, and I felt like I was going back in time as there were many old buildings still standing. My mind kept wandering back to the early sixties, visualising the old shops. Back then, it was a thriving street, bustling with people. Now, it seemed to have lost its vibrancy. If you look online, you'll see that Union Street was once full of hustle and bustle, but now, all that seemed to have gone.

It had been a long day. I was mentally drained and decided I was definitely having an early night, as my brain was fried. After getting something to eat, I thought I would start writing this chapter to reflect on how my journey had been so far.

My support coordinator from Future Pathways, Yvonne, arrived, and we discussed how I wanted to manage the day, focusing entirely on what I wanted to do. She knew how my mind worked, having supported me through many difficult times.

We went for coffee and decided to take a walk along the beach, which held fond memories for me. It was quite a cold and miserable day, but I remembered the beach as a vibrant place in the early to mid-sixties, full of people enjoying the sun and all the beach had to offer. Kids were building sandcastles, paddling at the water's edge, and generally having fun.

The beach had a darker memory for me as well though.

CHAPTER 21:
NOT ALL BEACH DAYS ARE SUNNY DAYS

We were informed one particular morning that we were going to the beach. It was a bright summers day, and the sky was blue as can be, with cotton like clouds across the sky hovering in waiting for the sun to shine through. The weather always made a difference to me giving me hope that somehow that day would be better than the previous one. On this particular day, unknown to me it would change my life in so many ways and impact my life to add shame guilt and mental health issues.

I woke up as usual that morning, and like most mornings, I had wet the bed. I knew immediately what was ahead, a punitive routine of harsh punishment and humiliation. Its hard to describe what goes through a young child's head when they know exactly what's coming. I of course had numbed to the process even though it was still very frightening to go through. I always was full of fear and trepidation, which never really left me.

Later that morning, we were informed we were going to the beach. I was very excited even though I had endured what had gone on earlier that morning and was still feeling the effects of the cold bath and being scrubbed by Jayes fluid and carbolic soap. I realise now that on many occasions, I had the ability to disassociate myself from what was happening around me to help cope with the reality of my life.

It was the summer holidays, and everyone was off school; when we did go to the beach, we usually left mid-morning, so we were there for most of the day. As a young child, anything that distracted me from my reality was exciting, We all helped make the sandwiches, they were usually filled with sandwich paste and were not very tasty - in fact they were awful - nonetheless we all helped prepare them and put them in Fyffes old cardboard boxes and load them into the minibus .

The minibus was driven by what I perceived as an old man probably around fifty five or sixty years of age, very tall and quite intimidating in stature who always wore a long dark coat and had the smell of alcohol on his breath. On reflection I'm surprised no-one ever seemed to notice or actually say anything about it. He was very scary and didn't really say much. He was an employee and he was just responsible for driving the minibus.

On this particular day we loaded up the minibus with the sandwiches, kettle and boxes of fruit, and we departed for the beach.

I knew the route well, we drove along Claremont Street turned left on to Grattan Place then right on to Union Grove a street - that was a very long one filled with what I thought, as a child, as the posh houses built with grey granite. At the end of Union

Grove we turned left on to Holburn Street and shortly later bared right on to the infamous bustling Union Street which cut its way right through the city to Castlegate. Then crossing over King Street, then eventually on to Beach Boulevard, which took you to the beach promenade.

I had made this journey so many times and had observed so much, staring through the window of the bus as a young child, remembering all the street names. I knew we were halfway there when we reached C&A, a clothing store on the right-hand side of Union Street.

Aberdeen Beach was a beautiful beach, with miles of golden sands and breakers sectioning off parts of the beach. As we approached, I remember the shows on the right-hand side, another name for the Carnival, full of bright lights, bumper cars, candy floss, toffee apples and the infamous waltzers and helter-skelter - a million miles from my usual world.

Immediately approaching the beach, you could see in the distance the Aberdeen baths, a prominent red brick building with a large chimney, which housed the swimming baths. I always found this very odd to have a swimming bath at the beach, nevertheless Aberdeen had one since 1898 until it closed in 1972.

On arrival, we made our way down the concrete steps down onto the promenade at the bottom. It was always jam-packed on sunny days, I could always smell calamine lotion just outside the medical centre that was located there. We passed the ice cream kiosk with its bright red roof, where people were queuing up. Then we walked by the children's playpen on the beach and along to the small hut where we could change. My excitement building all the time in anticipation of a perfect fun packed day at the beach.

Once we arrived, we got changed and made our way down to the beach. As you can imagine, it was a place of escapism for a young child like me. All my thoughts, fears, and anxieties seemed to disappear. I had many adventures over many years, enjoying the bustling activities along the beach.

This particular day was like most days we spent on the beach, building sandcastles, getting covered in sand everywhere and doing what most children do - paddling at the water's edge, jumping the waves as the tide came in and generally having fun. Later we had our sandwiches and tea and a piece of fruit.

Little did I know that, like the beginning of my day, the end of my day would end in such a traumatic experience that would affect and impact my life in years to come. We packed up and made our way back to the minibus, my short escape from reality had come to an end.

When we returned and unloaded everything, I was directed to help the driver clean the bus. I grabbed a broom and went to the back of the bus, sweeping all the sand out from the corners.

I already felt uncomfortable being left alone with the driver, as he was very intimidating. There was something scary about him.

As I was completing the task of cleaning and brushing the bus out, I sensed something wasn't quite right. I could feel it in my gut. This old man had been staring at me throughout which raised my adrenalin levels. I was full of absolute fear and anxiety. I hesitantly stepped out of the rear of the bus almost in anticipation of something happening.

He immediately grabbed my arm and my worst fear came to fruition. He dragged me around to the other side of the vehicle. By this time pure fear was running through my veins as I was begging him to let me go. Tears flooding my eyes.

My request fell on deaf ears as he ignored my pleas, telling me to shut up and be quiet.

By this time fear had engulfed my small body and I just froze in absolute terror not knowing what was happening.

He began fondling me and I begged him again to stop. Then, to my surprise, he did. However, he then grabbed my hand as he unzipped his trousers and physically forced my hand on to him to do something I knew nothing about as a child.

I stared into the concrete wall opposite the bus. I totally shut down and disassociated myself from what was happening as if I wasn't there. Now silent tears running down my face.

I was a young child, confused and full of fear. I didn't understand what was happening but I knew it was wrong. I had no control over it at all. I was being controlled through fear and power. It was like an out of body experience as I subconsciously removed myself from reality.

Once it was over, an overwhelming sadness and hurt came over me. I was full of anger shame and guilt. I felt every emotion going, as if I was to blame and had done something wrong. Even back then I knew that day would affect me for the rest of my life.

You can never underestimate the impact any sort of abuse has on any child and how profoundly it affects them. That particular day was probably the worst day of my life as it had so many highs and lows from the time I woke up having wet the bed and the fear I felt in knowing what was coming, the humiliation, the punches, followed by a cold bath and being scrubbed by Jayes Fluid. Then, I was taken to the beach, where I got a short respite from my reality and finished my day being abused by someone who took advantage of my young age and vulnerability - instilling fear, threat, confusion, anger, shame, and an overwhelming hurt and sadness that I will never get over.

I will always remember, sadly, beach days didn't mean sunny days!

.oOo.

For over half a century, I had always kept the fact I had been sexually abused as a child to myself. For years, I kept it hidden, too embarrassed to talk about it, too ashamed to disclose it to anyone. Even to the point I didn't have the courage to disclose it at the Scottish Abuse Inquiry. I felt there was such a stigmatisation attached to sexual abuse, and - at that particular time - I just wasn't ready. I found it a lot easier to disclose physical and emotional abuse, but there is something very difficult in talking about sexual abuse and how it has impacted your life.

Writing this book has helped me navigate my thoughts, feelings, and emotions around it. I remember the day I decided to tell my daughter Ashleigh what had happened. I was full of trepidation and anxiety. We were both in her kitchen, and I found the right words. We both cried that day and hugged each other. It was a special moment that I will never forget.

CHAPTER 22:

LEAVING THE PAST BEHIND

Seeing the beach again in 2024 was different. It was early spring, but it was nothing like I remembered. I was almost disappointed as memories came flooding back. I recognised some places, like the steps I would have walked down as a child, the smell of calamine lotion in the air, but there was no ice cream kiosk, no beach huts, no playpen on the beach. It had lost its appeal.

Clearly, there had been little investment in the promenade or surrounding area, which was quite sad to see. I concluded that I would rather hold on to my happy days of sheer escapism, of sandcastles and ice cream covered in sand, and paddling at the beach with the North East wind blowing in my hair as a child. It was interesting to reflect on how the past and present can impact you. Ironically, I'd rather save the past images in my memories, as the beach now appeared to have no heart.

The time had come to visit the place where I had been brought up and had left forty-nine years earlier. We made our way through the grey streets of Aberdeen, eventually arriving at Claremont Street. We pulled up in the car, and I had no idea how I would feel or what emotions would come my way. There must have been some deep-rooted feeling, as my eyes filled with tears and I became emotional, realising where I was.

Memories came flooding back. We got out of the car and made our way to the right-hand gate. Immediately, I realised the gate was not as big as I remembered. What surprised me was the sheer size of the Nazareth House building. As an adult, it shocked me how big it was. It made me think about the impact it must have had on me as a child. I felt scared and overwhelmed.

There were moments as I walked around the building where I placed myself fifty-odd years ago. I stood at the rear of the building, exactly where I would have been on my red tricycle, riding around the concrete playground, now a car park, staring up at the imposing structure. I pointed out where the bathrooms were, where we were thrown into cold baths full of Jeyes fluid and scrubbed because we were "dirty."

As we made our way back to the front, there were a row of quaint bungalows that had been built. I worked out they had replaced the outhouse where the minibus had been parked all those years ago, where the driver had abused me as a very young child. All sorts of emotions went through my body as I walked past. But at that moment, although emotional, I was proud of myself. Proud that despite the odds, I had survived.

For someone to survive historical abuse and tell their story, it takes a lot of courage and resilience. Opening up wounds that had been closed for many years is never easy. I hope my story gives people hope that they can come to terms with their past and remind them they are important, loved, and believed. My healing shadows are still healing; whether they will ever fully heal is questionable. But my journey needed to be completed. A part of me probably died within those walls many years ago but enduring it all made me a very empathetic person, regardless of my own hurt.

Hopefully, after completing this book, I will finally find peace in the latter years of my life and draw a line under that part of my life. I can only hope.

I stood in the spot as an adult where, sixty-one years earlier, I had sat on a small red tricycle, looking up at the building the same way I had so many years before. I thought of my life and the journey I had come through. There were many difficult and painful memories, but at the end of the day, I had survived and come back to reclaim my life. It brought up a wealth of emotions but was a turning point for me. I had reservations about going there, but the sense of empowerment was undeniable.

I was there—I hadn't let the cycle continue. I am a good person despite what they did to me. I like the word resilience and what it means to an individual. People can overcome trauma—they have that ability in them. No matter what they threw at me, I am still here to tell the story, and I do have a sense of pride that through all the trauma and confusion, I somehow managed to survive. I gave myself a pat on the back.

There are days that make all the difference—that little boy on the bike didn't know he had twelve years ahead of him, filled with shame and guilt. But at the end of the day, I am still here, telling my story. Everyone's journey through trauma is different; it is an individual experience in how you recover. If you are 1% further forward and feeling better after a visit like mine, then you are moving forward and away from the trauma itself.

EPILOGUE:
TRIGGERED

I've always been fascinated by how the mind has the ability to compartmentalise the past into metaphorical boxes in the recesses of our memory. It can keep thoughts and emotions locked away for years, under control, until one day, for whatever reason, it can no longer hold them there. When this happens, it's as if the floodgates of emotion are opened, and they become all-consuming and overwhelming. In a flash, your past revisits you, sometimes with no warning, and I have learned how crippling that can be.

Writing this book has been a journey, sometimes a very painful one. I have been triggered many times in recounting my past, but there is something cathartic about putting your own words down about your own individual thoughts and feelings. It has been a way to process how my past has impacted my life. Occasionally, I've wondered if it was worth the mental strain it has put me under. Yet, I always concluded that I wouldn't change anything at all; it has all been part of my journey, hopefully leading to healing. I believe my past holds the key to my healing. As the title "Healing Shadows" suggests, the shadows of my past, though not fully revealed, have initiated my healing process. By talking and writing about my past, the shadows of my hurt and pain that I carried for years have started to lift.

Everyone's journey is different, and I'm often asked why I chose to bring up the past, let alone write about it. My simple answer is that I felt it would help me and, hopefully, others who have been through childhood trauma. I have been damaged by my past, but I hope that writing this helps me and others navigate their journeys. I will never get my childhood back, but by writing this, I hope it opens up discussions about mental health and why people may act in certain ways.

Everyone has a story to tell. If we all had a more empathetic and kinder outlook towards people struggling with mental health, the world would definitely be a better place. Cliché as that sounds, it's very true.

A few years ago, I was diagnosed with Complex Post-Traumatic Stress Disorder. This diagnosis helped me understand why I struggled in life. Writing this book gave me a sense of purpose and identity, helping me navigate my emotions. It was very triggering at times. Although I probably didn't realise how much it would be, it brought back the night terrors, the cold sweats in the middle of the night, and, of course, my old friend insomnia.

At times, I fell into my old friend depression and the black clouds loomed ominously, feeling extremely low and drinking again. Of course, this just made things worse. I had lost good friends in this process because the impact of my drinking and how much writing the book triggered me brought old habits of using alcohol to self-medicate. Sometimes my thought process and behaviour were quite bizarre, and I genuinely wasn't in control of those thoughts and emotions. I went through a few crises, wondering why I was putting myself through this turmoil. I sometimes doubted myself, wondering if I was doing the right thing. Many friends and family praised me, telling me I was doing the right thing despite my self-doubt. One thing I have learned is how powerful the mind can be with its ability to store memories, whether good or bad, and also lock away memories that you don't want to think about. Somehow, they can be triggered.

I'm sure there are more positives than negatives in writing this book. It helped me come to the decision that my drinking days were completely over. The good thing was I was never reliant on alcohol, although I did use it as a coping mechanism to deal with my thoughts and emotions that were already all over the place. My only regret is that I didn't properly decide earlier. I had made sound bites that I was going to bring an end to my drinking days, probably realising that it wouldn't happen. So, I had to take a level of responsibility and accept that alcohol, mental health, and childhood trauma most definitely do not go together. I was becoming more of a liability, certainly not thinking straight and being overly hypersensitive to anything and anyone, paranoid about all sorts of things. So, the decision to genuinely go teetotal from here on in was a no-brainer in the end. It should have been made a long time ago. Although it was a difficult decision, it was the right decision for me. Once I made that decision, I felt a total sense of relief within myself. Deep down, I wanted to have an alcohol-free life, stop being a party animal, and, more importantly, stop falling out with my friends and waking up the next morning with "the fear" and be clear-headed. The trouble with me was that I was a binge drinker. I could go weeks without touching alcohol, then bang—once I did, I hit it and hit it hard.

I found it difficult to express what I was going through to people. I was constantly living on the edge with anxiety that crippled me. I didn't want to mix with people other than a few close friends. Not only was it difficult for me, but I'm sure for them too. I suppose it's difficult for people to try and understand my triggering thoughts and emotions, mood swings, anxiety, and emotional dysregulation, especially when I myself didn't understand how to manage those emotions. Yes, I knew for years that I had emotional dysregulation, and most of the time, I sort of managed it, but when I started writing this book, it went off the scale and impacted a few close friends.

All I can do now is try and heal—another new journey with no alcohol in my life and counselling using cognitive behaviour therapy to help me manage my emotions. Another difficult journey, but one I hope will help. I think throughout my life, I have realised I lost a part of me throughout my childhood. It's sad that it's taken sixty-three years of my life to get to this point.

Today, as an adult, I still grapple with the deep-seated shame and guilt instilled in me during those formative years. The memories of abuse and humiliation are ever-present, shadows that haunt me. Yet, despite the darkness, I have found a way to survive, to push through the pain and emerge with a resilience that defines who I am.

This resilience is a testament to the human spirit's capacity to endure, to find light even in the darkest of times. My journey is one of survival, of overcoming unimaginable adversity, and finding strength within. It is a journey that continues, one step at a time, towards healing and reclaiming my sense of self-worth.

ACKNOWLEDGEMENTS

Firstly, I would like to Thank Future Pathways, the organisation set up by the Scottish Government to support survivors of abuse in the Scottish Care System. Without their funding, this would never have been possible.

I would also like to say a special thanks to the lovely, kind, understanding, and empathetic Yvonne Donald, my Support Coordinator from Future Pathways, who believed in me in writing this book. She has given me a wealth of support for the last few years and to whom I will always be indebted for helping me navigate my thoughts, feelings, and emotions through good and bad times.

I would also like to say a massive thanks to the lovely Mary Turner Thomson, best-selling author, for giving me the encouragement, guidance, and belief that I could write this book. Your empathetic nature and support in helping me edit this book were unwavering. Your ability to listen and help me through this process, and your encouraging words and belief will never leave me.

To my Family and close friends who stood by me through the good, the bad, and the ugly, thank you. I'll never forget.

To my daughter Ashleigh, who has been with me every step of the way in writing this book, I thank you for the unwavering support, understanding, and love you have shown me throughout this process. I'm so very proud of you.

Last but by no means least, thank you to all those abuse survivors who gave evidence to The Scottish Abuse Inquiry; please remember you are important, that you are enough, and you ARE believed.